Cars, Castles, Cows,and Chaos

A New Jersey Girl's Humorous Romp Throughout Italy

By
Midge Guerrera

with illustrations by
Janet Cantore-Watson

D0731486

Published by

Read Furiously
Read Often. Read Well.

Read (v): The act of interpreting and understanding the written word.

Furiously (adv): To engage in an activity with passion and excitement.

**Read Often. Read Well.
Read Furiously**

Table of Contents

Author's Note

This book is a memoir and reflects mini moments in my life. Some names and characteristics have been changed, some events have been compressed and others elongated. The stories and dialogue have been embellished and recreated. Some Italian has been italicized to establish a specific tone.

Prologue

It was a tree that broke this camel's back. One morning we woke up to yet another storm-felled giant tree on our New Jersey lawn. Another fallen, thousand-dollar-to-remove-it tree. We groaned at what we knew would be our fifth thousand-dollar tree removal phone call, looked at each other and said, "Let's sell the bloody house."

My, that sounds spontaneous and frankly, a bit insane.

The next day a contract was signed and the house was on the market. The house that had been in my Italian family for close to a century. On the market meant the bits and pieces of my family history stored in barns, attics, the basement and sheds had to be sorted, catalogued, cried over and let go. The house, we had totally renovated, loved but since retiring spent less and less time in, sold in one week. *Gulp.*

The buyer wanted to close in a month. *Gulp, gulp.*

Crushed into a ten-by-ten-foot storage unit was stuff we couldn't live without. We sold everything else, including cars, clothes, furniture – everything. Yes, you can empty a two-hundred- and fifty-year-old farmhouse, barns and garages in a month. We contracted a company that transformed our home into a two-story market. Each room became its own little shop – clothes shop, collectables shop, tool shop, art gallery, furniture warehouse.

People came, bought and carried our New Jersey history away with them. At the end of the three-day sale, the dregs of our lives remained floating on the terraces, hidden in barns and tossed in the basement. What to do? Hmm, what you can't sell you give away. I had given away books, clothes, and furniture via Freecycle.org for years. That method requires giving away one item at a time. I had a pazillion items and the clock was ticking. I looked at a barn and wondered if I could do a spin on a well-advertised garage sale. No money exchanges hands and everybody walks away with something. I invented the *Free Sale* and had hundreds of folks lining up for a chance to trek through our barn and take whatever they could carry out.

I posted ads on all the garage sale websites, in the newspaper and of course illegally on telephone poles. At 8:00 AM on the morning of the *Free Sale*, balloons marked the end of our driveway and signs guided drivers to the parking field. The event was to run from 9:30 AM until 2:00PM.

At 8:05 AM the first car pulled in.

At 8:06 the second car parked and blocked the driveway. I went to the first driver and explained we weren't opening until 9:30. The woman, with a gaggle of kids in the car, told me her daughter was destitute and needed anything she could find – couldn't she please look first? The second car was obviously manned by an antique dealer. He smiled and asked to just have a little peak to see if it was worthwhile.

I said, "Sure, anything you find costs $100 to take away."

"What! This is advertised as a Free Sale and all must go."

"Yup, at 9:30 everything is free. At 8:10 everything costs $100."

"Do you have place tickets?" Place tickets? I figured we would be lucky if 3 people came.

I smiled and said, "Of course I have place tickets in the house. I'll be right back – and don't open the barn door!"

I raced into the soon-not-to-be my house, scrounged up a

pad of paper and started cutting little squares. I numbered one through ten and ran back out to the drive. After handing driver number one who was still looking sadly at the barn, ticket number 1, I handed ticket number 2 to the dealer. Off they went, promising to return. I numbered up to 20 and thought that was optimistic.

By 9:15 AM the parking field was packed and I had given out 100 tickets! People were lined up down our long driveway. They were getting antsy. My theatre brain kicked in and I started entertaining. Laughter quelled the beast. I made up rules on the spot. Rules that absolutely worked:

1. I would let people into the barn in groups of 5 and they had five minutes to find their treasures. I sounded a bell at the end of five minutes.
2. Only adults were allowed in the barn.
3. They could only take what they could carry out. (People became very creative using all sorts of things as carryalls – the rusted milking pail came out filled with a rolled throw rug balancing through the handles.)
4. Once they carried out a load, they got a new ticket and went to the end of the line.

Groans went up, but everyone was eager to play. I had called for reinforcements. My sister raced over and set up a play area for kids. My pal, Janet, worked the line making balloon animals. Cousin Maryellen set up a boombox and got folks dancing. I rang a bell and the first five raced in. People took stuff that I would have paid someone to take to the dumps. Shovel bottoms without handles, cat carrier missing the door, jars of rusted nails, faded political signs from the 1960s and every last piece of anything in that barn. By noon the barn was broom clean. *Whish*, everything went in a couple of carnival-like hours. Even though it took a day out of my life, it saved me the cost of a dumpster!

Afterwards, I sipped a Scotch and stared at the now empty parking field. I asked my husband, Jack: "Now what?"

Having talked about retiring in Italy and having no place to go in New Jersey, it seemed prudent to test Italy out. We rented a place in Pontelandolfo, Italy for four months. Why this tiny little hilltop town in Campania? Pontelandolfo is my ancestral village and when I walk the hills, I feel my nonna walking beside me. In 1995, I had done a lot of genealogical research in the village's municipal building. We found my dad's first cousins. Cousins that he didn't know existed. They embraced us and we continued to visit them almost every year for fifteen years. We would stay a few days, then a week, then two weeks and then once dragged by dad along and rented an apartment for a month. We loved the town and the people.

Figuring out what we would do after a four-month foray into Italy wasn't on my checklist. That's what sisters and cousins are for! Couch surfing for pensioners! Are we insane?

Am I insane?

Don't answer that.

The four months were just a teaser. Waking up to the fresh air and walking down the hill to the piazza for the ninety-cent cappuccino and conversation was a game changer. Jack and I adored our new landlords and the incredibly low price we paid for a huge house. We promptly signed a year-round lease on the house and have been spending half of the year in Southern Italy ever since.

La Dolce Vita – the sweet life…

…or is it?

Year
One

The Car Rental

Rat-ta-tat-tat-rat-ta-tat-tat-tttttaat - my brain was firing on all pistons. A stream of incoherent expletives in two languages shot out of my mouth and echoed through our otherwise empty house. How the hell was I going to get everything done?

My list was short but not simple:

- House to rent for four months – check, done.
- Pack and ship clothes to Italy for four months – check, done.
- Car rental – CAR RENTAL for four months in Southern Italy - **#$%^&@**. There is no check, done! Will there ever be a check, done? How will I get it done? *Errrrrrgggggg*.

I know what you are thinking – what is she **$%^&@**-ing about? People on vacation rent cars every day. Easy-peasy – walk out of the airline terminal, go to a big corporate car rental agency and rent a car. **NOT!**

Not if you are staying in Italy for longer than 2 minutes and want to be able to pay for anything else.

Not if your Italian family will roll their eyes, gnash their teeth and scream at you for paying too much.

Not if you will be fighting with your husband about the size, color and zip of the rental options.

Not if the plan is to save money by living in the village of your ancestors where a delicious cappuccino costs only 90 cents.

Long term car rentals cost un sacco di soldi. We didn't have a sack of cash. The cheapest places we found – that year – were averaging €400 a week for a - *honk, honk* - baby clown car. Multiply that times 16 weeks – gulp, €6400 – even more in U.S. dollars. We were a bit flummoxed and needed some advice. I started asking the experts – our cheap traveling grasshopper pals who, like us, want to figure out how to get over on Big Corporations and still live the good life.

One Italo-Americano friend had the perfect solution: "Go to a local car dealer and rent a used car off the lot. Oh, just make sure you take someone who knows the guy."

What a great idea! I called my peeps in Italy and asked if anyone knew a friendly local used car dealer. I was told not to worry. It would be handled. What would we do without our Italian family and friends who are like family?

The jet-lagged day we arrived in Pontelandolfo, I stayed in our new home to unpack. Jack and our friend "who knows a guy" headed out towards Benevento to pick up our cheapo rental car from an auto dealer. Let's call our friend Guido and the dealer Furbo. (That Italian word, *furbo*, is defined as "sly, cunning, shrewd.") Guido drives Jack through the winding back roads of Campania to pick up the car at Furbo's dealership.

When they arrived, Furbo looked at Jack. Then he looked at our friend and said, "lui non parla italiano? Questo è un problema."

Nope, Jack didn't speak Italian. But, hey, what was the problem? The auto dealer never spoke directly to him again. Furbo gabbed on and on like Jack wasn't even there. He never looked at him or acknowledged him.

Suddenly, the dealer got up and got in the car. Guido nodded and stood. Jack and Guido leaped in Guido's car and followed Furbo at a quick clip around S curves and over railroad tracks. Jack, using his face, hands and limited Italian, discovered the dealer was driving the car we would rent and leading them to a bar for coffee. Jack, having worked abroad, thought *un caffè* was part of negotiations. Nope. Not here. No negotiations between renter and owner – nada, nothing. Though at one point, Furbo did talk to Jack – he asked him if he wanted *un caffè*.

Time to pay – Jack brought out his credit card. The force of the malocchio coming from Furbo was fierce. That evil eye knocked Jack back three feet and turned his hair white.

Gulp, who knew we had to pay in cash? *ERRRRGGGG*, we should have known! Most of Southern Italy is a cash society with a lot of that cash soldi in nero – under the table. The dealer's frown turned to a big bad wolf smile and he nodded to someone.

Non c'è problema.

Not a problem, the dealer's family owned the gas station next door. (They probably owned the caffè, coffee distribution and gas delivery trucks too.) A really old man was leaning on the pumps with his arms crossed and staring at Jack through two piercing blue eyes. He had been watching the bar and must have gotten a secret signal. He bent his pointer finger at Jack and then at the pump shack. Jack got up, looked around for help and carried over his credit card.

The man – I'm guessing Furbo's papà - ran the card through for the whole €1500 rental. (Note €1500 versus €6400.) For that bargain price, we got an older small gray

Fiat to use for four months. When the dealer gave Jack the keys, he pointed at the gas gauge – it was empty. Jack gave the old man at the pumps back his card and now smiling, the old man filled up the tank. Ciao was said by all. Furbo left. Jack, with our rental, followed Guido back to Pontelandolfo.

Notice anything strange about this transaction?

Think about it. Did they ask Jack for his passport? No.

Did they ask to copy his driver's license? No.

Did they ask him to sign any papers? No.

Did they ask if he wanted insurance? No.

Did they ask where he would be staying in Italy? Did they even ask him his name? No and no.

Jack realized they had no idea who he was or where the car was going. (Well, they did have his credit card number.) Actually, renting a car was easy-peasy. For what it would cost normally for a week's luxury car rental at the airport we had a little grey Fiat for four months. Hell, no paperwork, no title, no insurance. We never changed the oil or put air in the tires. All we did was gas it up.

Oh yeah, and I named it Topo Grigio – grey mouse. It squeaks but it keeps on running. The day we left Italy, we left Topo Grigio at our house and someone retrieved it. Done.

Back in the States, as I was telling the story, I realized that the car may not have even been theirs. But hey, what is a stolen car among friends? Viva L'Italia!

Stick Shifts, Parking, and Gas Olio

I toss the gear into reverse, ease off the clutch and pound on the gas. The car bucks, hops, lunges and stalls. I blame our creepy, little Topo Grigio. I mean, driving a car with a standard transmission is just like riding a bike or having sex. It is something you remember how to do no matter how long it's been since the last time you did it. Thank the goddesses, I am alone in the blasted car. I will try again. This time I am painfully slow. I release the clutch so slowly, that my left leg starts to tremble. My leaden right foot takes a breath and my big toe lightly, lightly steps on the gas. The car starts to back up the driveway. I smile. Topo Grigio burps and we are off on our first trip together to Piazza Roma.

Standard transmission cars are all we see here. The local men playing cards in front of the bars gasp in amazement when I buckle up for safety on the driver's side. Some bellow, "Where's Jack?" I wave and start to drive away. I know what they are thinking: "Americans don't drive standards. Who is this crazy woman? Get out of her way!"

This crazy woman started driving a standard transmission vehicle when she was ten. Seriously, it only took me a nanosecond to remember how to do it smoothly and with aplomb.

(Jack just read this and reminded me that my nanosecond was about two days.)

I don't know about other women, but I learned to drive when I was three, during the unsafe 1950's, by sitting on my dad's lap and steering the car. I think I was actually steering too. Impossible you think? By the time any kid growing up in rural New Jersey on a mini farm could ride a bike, they were on the back of an ancient, held-together-with-baling-wire tractor. The only way I knew how to drive was jamming on the clutch, moving the big black knob attached to the stick on the floor and stomping on the gas. Buck the car much – sure. But hey, by the time I was twelve, I had it down. Literally, by the time I was twelve, in an emergency, I had driven my mother home. We had a tiny Simca – which I discovered recently was an offshoot of Fiat. It was old, tiny and white. Obviously, it provided an early lesson for driving Topo Grigio.

The only thing I wasn't so good at here in Pontelandolfo was making it up perpendicular hills. Do I stay in first gear, even though poor Topo Grigio was panting, or try to nudge it into second? Shifting meant for a moment I wasn't in complete control of the car. What if I didn't give it enough gas? What if it started to roll backwards?

No *what ifs* – please don't tell anyone, but it happened. The car stalled and rolled, rolled and rolled back down the hill.

"Merde!!!!!"

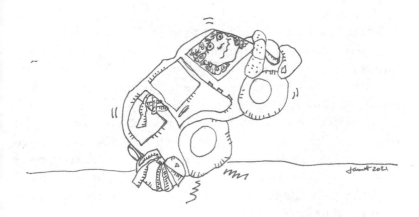

Meanwhile, I was biting my lip, turning the key, slamming it into first and stamping on the gas.

I am now happy cruising up the hill at a snail's pace. Ooops – there was one other thing I wasn't so good at: parking. Fitting even a small Fiat into an even smaller space on a hill while staring straight up at the sky is nerve wracking.

"Why are those black and white birds flying near the windshield peering in at me?"

Reverse, turn the wheel, stare in the mirror. First gear, turn the wheel the other way and pray no one is watching. Jam this car into that spot and don't roll backwards no matter what. The first time I parked, I forgot to turn my tires out or in (hmmm…which is it?). As I started to get out of the car, the car started a slow roll backwards. Emergency brake be damned – did I use it? I leaped in, pulled on the brake and turned the wheels in or out. If I just kept them pointing straight ahead – perfect for rolling straight down the hill if the hand brake fails – I'd be in deep doo doo.

Happily, Topo Grigio, managed to never roll away on me. That said, parking is a new cultural experience.

My cousin commanded, "Just pull across the street and park there."

"What? That's the wrong direction."

"Look – all those cars are pointed in the wrong direction."

"I can't do it," I squealed.

"Yes, you can! Just pull over there. This is Italy."

That discussion happened more than once until I got it into my thick skull that this was Southern Italy and there are no parking rules. Folks just stop their cars and leave them. The rest of us drive around them.

During big events, our Piazza Roma becomes a parking lot that would drive an organized person insane. Cars are pointed in all directions. Cars block other cars. Cars are so close together that only a snake could wiggle into the door. The chaos made me crazy until the ever-calm Jack pointed out that whenever we wanted to leave, we could leave.

True, if we were blocked in and pointed at our car, voices would shout for the blocking car's owner and the offending car would be moved. If we needed to run into the Mini Market, I could just leave the car in the middle of the road and people would drive around me too. Woo woo – pretty cool.

Filling the car with fuel for the first time was another traumatic experience. Remember, Jack had filled it up when he rented the car. It ran for almost a month on that one tank. The fuel gauge was in the red zone and I started to get nervous.

First panic attack: which side of the car is the little door on? Whew, I remembered all cars have a little arrow for us dummies on the gauge. Easy. I looked: It was on the passenger side.

Second panic attack: this one was a doozy. I pulled over and ransacked the glove box looking for the car's manual. Like Mary Poppins's satchel, more and more junk kept appearing and falling on the floor. Cripes, is that someone's thesis from university? When the glove box was empty, I started to cry. There was no manual. What kind of fuel does this stupid car take?

Do you know how many types of fuel you can get for a car here in Italy? No, not just leaded, unleaded and diesel. These Italians are way ahead of us in the alternative energy field. Try G.P.L (liquified propane), Metano (Methane Gas – is that from cow poop?), Gasolio (diesel), BluDiesel (super clean diesel), Benzina senza piombo (unleaded gas), and BluSuper (higher octane unleaded). Did I forget anyone? Oh yeah, electric vehicles.

This is an old car, I thought. It can't use one of the eco smart fuels – could it? I stared out the window and started the car. What is the worst that can happen? I get embarrassed because I pull up to the wrong tank? I feel totally stupid because the tanks at our local station don't have the type of fuel I need? Who cares? Quest'è Italia!

I pull into Pontelandolfo's only station. Pietro looks at the car and at me. I smile. He signals I should go to the other side of the tank. Rats, I had even looked at the damn arrow.

Whew! I picked the right kind of fuel – gasolio. Really, I had no idea what was in that tank until after he filled it and I read the sign. Diesel – the little grey rented Fiat uses plain old diesel.

After those initial moments of panic, the car and I got

along famously. It didn't talk back or punk out and I didn't kick it, curse or cry. We both just smiled along the roads in the Sannio Hills.

Don't Drive in Naples

"Watch out! Sheeeeeeeet, the motorini is aiming for us." I clutch the armrest. My heart races.

Jack scowls and bellows, "STOP SCREECHING!"

"Ahhhhh, thank you for listening. I have discharged my angst." I inhale deeply, and count to ten. "Hmmmmmmmm."

I visualize white light surrounding the car. "WATCH OUT!!!!!!" I immediately stop all this relaxation, funky granola bullshit and bellow, "DON'T EVER TAKE A FREAKIN' CAR INTO THE CENTER OF NAPLES AGAIN!"

I better start at the beginning. That first year, in our little Topo Grigio, we decided to take advantage of a sun-filled day and further explore Naples. We had gone a few weeks earlier with our landlord, Nicola. It was our first opportunity to see the city that was once the international seat of arts, culture and home to the oldest state university in the world – Università degli Studi di Napoli Federico II. Nicola drove us directly into the glorious historic center. He was incredibly familiar with the city and assured us that the historic center was clean, safe and wonderful. It was - the architecture and history are worth a visit. With Nicola leading the way, we strolled down to the waterfront, had a caffè in a small bar and people watched.

We thought, after that great first experience, we could visit Naples on our own.

(Notice: "we thought")

The downside of idyllic, very small village life is that there is really no decent public transportation. At 7:00 or 7:40 AM, students and those lucky enough to have jobs can take the bus to our provincial capital, Benevento. From there you can take a train or bus to other places. One can take that same bus all the way to Naples...at 7:00 in the morning? We weren't going to do that.

Our original plan was to take the train from Benevento. Great plan: twenty-minute ride to the station in a car we know can get that far, thirty minutes trying to figure out where to park, and then finding a parking lot only to discover that the broken prepay machine only took coins! If we don't pay, we knew the parking gods would rain tickets down on us. Shouting and cursing ensued – that was me. Jack did the scowl/sigh thing.

My young cousin, Giusy, who then attended the prestigious Università degli Studi di Napoli Federico II and was squished in the tiny Fiat's backseat, murmured, "Maybe we should just drive."

I mean, she lives in Naples.

How bad could it be? The car got us this far. How bad could it be? *How bad could it be?*

Now that is an interesting question.

Perhaps, I should point out that ten years earlier, the first and the last time Jack drove to Naples, we were going to the Museo di Capodimonte and National Galleries and got stuck in a horn blowing, knives flashing, traffic jam at a 1/2-mile-wide round-about circle. We were forced to crawl around the circle for about 45 minutes.

We had only gone about half-way around the huge thing

when Jack was able to ease off into a wide avenue. In less than one block, the wide two-way street had bottlenecked into a goat path. People had double parked or abandoned their cars on both sides of the street.

It was an impassable, drivers-screaming-and-horns-blaring NIGHTMARE.

Jack, Mr. Calm in a crisis, pulled the car onto the sidewalk and told us to get out. When in Rome or Naples do as .... We abandoned the car, took a cab to the museum and worried about driving later.

So, why are we here driving to Naples again? Are we stupid?

Unlike the many years earlier debacle, this time we had our handy iPhones and could use the GPS. We knew we wanted to explore the bayside Posillipo neighborhood. Getting into the city was a dream. We took the autostrada to the city and then followed the water all the way to Posillipo, a glamorous part of the city. Parking in a lot was easy – though again you could only use change. Since we figured we only needed three hours to stroll, eat lunch and stare at the sea, we managed to scrounge up enough coins.

The view from Posillipo of the Bay of Naples is amazing. We all agreed this was the neighborhood to live in. Gated private streets led to magnificent houses and apartment buildings. Sigh, anybody want to give me a scant million.

Sadly, old wee Topo Grigio, surrounded by Lamborghinis, was embarrassed to be parked there.

Strolling through the neighborhood, we discovered a restaurant with an incredible view. Reginella Ristorante was the type of eatery that brochures touting the charms of a seaside community are sure to mention. It was perched on the side of the cliff leading down to the majestic Bay of Naples. The Bay really does look like all those deep blue sea tourism photos!

Tables were set on a terrace overlooking the sea. Initially, the charming host sat us right next to the railing – ah, a glorious view! Giusy and I looked at each other – we were both turning green. All I saw was my life passing before my eyes as I fell off the side of the fifth story veranda and lay broken on the rocks below. With chattering teeth, we asked for another table. Once we were happily seated a bit further back, we concentrated on the incredible seafood. Delicious!

Those of you waiting for the other DON'T DRIVE shoe to drop: Hang on – here it comes.

After lunch we strolled a bit and took in the sights of the neighborhood. Most shops were closed. Even stores in the cities close for lunch and a nap, opening again at about 4:30. Sated from lunch and the fabulous view, we decided to head for the historic center and check out where Giusy attended university and lived.

Whaaaaaaa. Whaaaaaa. Nervous breakdown alert.

If you do not have a strong stomach for street chaos, stop reading.

We set the GPS for the address of the apartment, followed the bay and suddenly were told to turn left into Dante's third level of HELL. Thousands of Evel Knievels zoomed in and out of stop-and-go traffic on motorcycles, motorino and broomsticks. Cars double and triple parked, making streets impassable. The GPS didn't quite get street closings due to well who knows – it was Tuesday.

Where the hell was my Xanax?

Clutching the purse on my lap like a life jacket, I tried not to cry out every time a freakin' car or motorini cut us off or came careening toward us. My nails bit into my palms. Jack squared his waspy jaw and forged ahead. Forging ahead isn't the right phrase. Begging for life – that's a good phrase. Or crying for my mother – that's a good phrase. It was like driving a car in a full washing machine set to the spin cycle. *Bump, rrrrrt, squeak, ugggg* — HELL.

Giusy reminded us she always took the bus and walked and didn't really know the direct driving route to her apartment. (Gee, thanks now for the relevant information!) We saw the sign for a parking lot and whipped the car in. Relief! On foot, we enjoyed exploring the oldest state university in the world.

Time to go. We trudged to the parking lot - where being 8 minutes late, they charged us for an extra hour. Giusy argued like a trooper - or an Italian woman - and she won! They didn't charge us.

We gritted our teeth for the drive home. I couldn't watch as Jack tried to squeeze out of the garage to the street. We hadn't a clue how to get out of town and the GPS on our iPhone was obviously under a lot of stress.

We ended up by the docks — well, that was fun. At least our car can fit in here. Not TOO many cars jockeying for position. We sat inhaling exhaust for what felt like hours (Jack says it was only 30 minutes). The conversation in the car came to a dead halt. Since I wasn't allowed to make caustic comments or scream, it was very quiet. Somehow Jack got us out of the city and onto the highway. We all exhaled and enjoyed the mountains, farms and lush green that is the Italian countryside. Naples is truly a glorious city.

Take the bus.

Don Quixote and I

As the wind whips over the mountains of Campania, whirling dervishes dance madly in the noon day sun. One morning, on our way to the Naples airport, I screeched at Jack to pull over. He raised an eyebrow and kept on driving. Rats, how would I really get a glimpse of the thousands of windmills that peppered the mountain ridge if he didn't pull over? Now, in his defense: we are driving Topo Grigio, I am not Dulcinea and he might have been apprehensive about stopping and starting.

That was the first time I spied the windmills that are part of the onshore wind farms that earned Italy its one time standing as the world's sixth largest producer of wind power. I have no idea how wind power works but from a distance I see sentries posted on the tops of mountains; Sannio soldiers gazing down on the approaching Romans; tall, helmets pointed to the heavens and still bodies against the azure sky.

Seriously, when I first saw a palo eolico - wind turbine - I wasn't thinking, *Gee, how green and save-the-planet this is.* I was thinking, *Hear the sounds of the marching feet as the Roman army emerges over the crest of the hill.* Honestly, from a distance they look like advancing ramrod straight soldiers with pointed hats. Up close they are more like super giant stick figures.

Up close? H'mm, did she really drive up the mountain to get closer? Yes, by gum we did! Why? Because we could!

OK, if the truth be told, it was a chilly, dreary day and I was going to poke out my eyes with a pen if we didn't get in the car and do something. Anything – as long as it didn't cost a bundle of bucks and we didn't have to change out of comfy clothes.

My brain tumbled and rumbled, and soon bizarre suggestions spew forth like Vesuvius.

Anything meant chasing windmills.

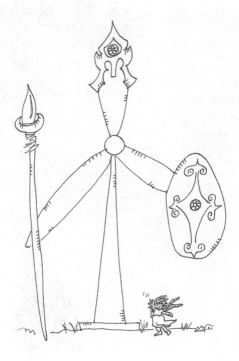

Jack, knowing divorce was imminent if he didn't get behind the wheel of the car, started the engine and let me navigate.

Navigation was something like – *NO, NO – TURN RIGHT* – whenever I saw the top of a windmill. We were so intent on getting close to the windmills that I didn't even shriek at the switchbacks along the way. What we didn't do was record exactly how to get to the ridge. All I remember was from Colle Sannita take SS 212 and make a right on SP 55. I was too entranced to take notes but remember saying at least 10 times – we are on SP55!

As we got closer, we saw bales of hay in fields around the windmills. Obviously, the farmers are still working their land. As we wended our way around, we passed beautiful new combines, tractors and balers. I guessed that the income from the utility companies helps keep this area green and farmed. Windmills plus farmland sure beats the housing developments plus loss of farmland that are a blight on New Jersey.

Up close and personal, I was a mini-David standing next to Goliath. The wind didn't ruffle my feathers, decapitated birds didn't fall on our heads. We did hear a kind of white noise *buzzzzzzzz*. That might annoy the hell out of me if I lived nearby. Not only were the structures majestic, but there was incredible architectural variety. Some looked like Eiffel Towers. I could hear Edith Piaf whispering a song in my ears. Others were powerful poles reaching to the heavens.

I learned something this grey day – chasing windmills is a guaranteed cure for boredom. Listen to the sound of the wind whistling on the ridge! Ah...

Stop!

One night, we wandered down towards Piazza Roma for an after-dinner drink or two at one of the outdoor bars. We love sitting outside and people watching. We only grasp about 20% of the conversations – mostly spoken in dialect – but it is great fun to play Harriet the Spy and listen in on the plots and twists of everyday life. Oops, Jack just looked over my shoulder and "ahhemed" – OK, OK, I'll drop the papal "we" - I'm the only one that eavesdrops on folks. We drove into town chatting away about the great meal we had just had that cost us about thirty dollars for two and included tons of food and booze, when...

Whoa – a police barricade had closed off access to the piazza.

Blinking lights and a temporary fence barred the way!

With burning brakes, we screeched to a halt, were detoured to a one-way street and wondered what was happening. Screams and shouts could be heard through our closed car windows. Was that fear? Could something heinous be happening – another revolution – the camerata knocking off the competition? I looked at Jack and knew we had to get closer and find out what was going on. He looked at me with that "sei pazzo?" (*are you crazy?*) expression. He suggested we turn around and go home. I suggested he wouldn't have a home if we didn't find out what was going on.

We parked near the town recycling bins – far enough away to be safe and close enough to hear the sounds. I hoped the garbage men didn't take Topo Grigio for scrap. As we walked, the cacophony of sound became clearer and clearer.

"Passa la palla!" (*Pass the ball!*)

"Che dici? Ma per chi tifi?" (*Are you serious? Whose side are you on?*)

"Cazzo!" (*F@#$!*)

"Ha preso la palla con entrambi i piedi!." (*He won the ball with both feet!*)

"Merda!" (*Shit!*)

"Il fallo!" (*Foul!*)

"Non posso credere che lo hai sbagliato!" (*Can't believe you missed that!*)

"Riggore adesso, adesso!" (*Penalty now, now!*)

"Caspita!" (*Wow!*)

Except for *caspita, merda* and *cazzo*, I didn't have a clue why or what people were yelling. Then screams turned into a wail – the piteous kind of forlorn wail that could only mean one possible thing in a small Italian town: some evil team scored a goal against Italy.

We rounded the corner and could see a movie screen set up in front of Bar 2000. The street was closed off, picnic tables filled the street and about a hundred people were gathered in front of a movie screen watching Italy and Brazil chase a soccer ball.

What a great marketing strategy for the bar! I asked around, curious to see if the town charged the bars for closing the street – a potential additional income stream. Why did people roll their eyes when I asked? Hey, it was a legitimate question. Jack cleared his throat. Then I remembered I had to stop thinking like an American.

That night, I finally began to understand calcio. Don't be silly, I still don't understand the rules or why a sport that is supposed to take 90 minutes takes a lot more than 90 minutes. What I finally began to understand was that the game wasn't as important as the opportunity for neighbors, friends, soon to be friends and outright enemies to have a communal focus. Joining the majority of the village in the Piazza that night, I saw everyone from infants to people older than Jack staring at movie screens and holding their collective breaths at the same time. Cries of alarm went up when goals were missed. Chairs were knocked over as the crowd leapt to its feet when a goal was made. In-between these specific moments people were talking to not only those at their table but to those around them.

People of all ages, from all neighborhoods, were enjoying the cool night air together. All Pontelandolfo had to do was put up a fence and a community event could be created.

We watched for a moment or two and walked the half a block to the next bar. There, a flat screen TV was perched on an outdoor bar tuned to the same game. A smaller but no less vocal crowd watched the game (or is that a match)? We stood there for a while too, adding our cheers, jeers and sighs to the sounds of the crowd. I mean after all it was just a typical night in a small Italian village.

When we finally left, the stanchions were down and you could drive through town. No one else seemed to care that the streets had been closed for calcio.

To Market, to Market to Buy a Fat Pig

Where did that nursery rhyme come from? I have never bought a fat pig. A faux Fendi purse, perhaps, but never a fat pig. Market day in Pontelandolfo is Wednesday - rain or shine the trucks pull in and set up shop. I will admit that when it really rains the number ranges from fewer to none. Every Wednesday you can buy fresh fish, fruit, vegetables, pillows, underwear, shoes, towels, clothes, purses, hats, baby chickens, plants, dog food, knives, rakes, hoes, furniture... well, you get the picture.

When we first came to Pontelandolfo over 25 years ago, the market had a different flavor - the high-tech trucks that flop open into stores are relatively new. I remember wine presses, rakes and dry goods dragged out of vans or three wheeled Ape trucks and displayed on folding tables or the ground.

On Wednesdays, I drive down to the piazza early to get a good seat to watch the set up. Some of these trucks are like giant transformer toys. *Whizzzzzzz, errrrrrrr, vrooooooom* – buttons are pushed and the sides of the trucks flip out as shelving units or racks of dresses *whirrrrrr* out. Amazing! For the price of a cappuccino (90 centesimi) I can sit and gape at the wonder of technology enhancing a system of sales that is thousands of years old.

Often, I watch the cars pull into the piazza and try to guess what kind of person owns that Mercedes, BMW, Volvo and even Jeeps. I know all the folks here who own Fiats, Lancias or Piaggio Ape. The fancy cars represent the city folks, upper middle-class neapolitan who buy up vacant mountain houses for weekend retreats. The market is no longer a lifeline to the outside world, but is now weekly entertainment. We all hunt for bargains, chat with pals and yelp with joy when we find something magical.

Prices here are less than the stores but for me they vary based on how well I speak Italian. My cousin bought a pair of stockings for €1. I raced up and asked for a pair and the vendor said €2. Oops, my accent was showing. I put them back and got Carmela to buy them for me. Can't blame the gal for wanting to make an extra buck - just not on me.

Each town has its own market day. That means I can hop in Topo Grigio, drive to a different place and check out that town's goodies, bars and restaurants. Big cities have ongoing markets. The market brings us back to our past when isolated villages depended on the itinerant vendors in their buggies bringing not only goods but word about the outside world. Most weeks now, the same trucks pull in. Father and son unpack and set up displays. I wonder how many of those fathers were once sons coming to this village with their fathers and father's father. (Not many women seem to be vending.) The sounds of the market are the same everywhere – joyful haggling, lilting and distinctive voices calling out the day's goods and, of course, the gossiping.

We have driven down the mountain to Benevento's market. Now that market is HUGE! It takes place at the soccer stadium. Soccer is this country's lifeblood and Benevento has its own team. The stadium parking lot holds a pazillion cars or a pazillion vendors. We parked Topo Grigio far away from the maddening crowd – well on the access road – and walked in.

I need a new purse. This one – no - that one. It was impossible to make up my mind. I never saw so many people selling "real" Gucci, Versace, Louis Vuitton and just about every contemporary designer. (Don't tell my niece Alex, but the designer wear she gets for Christmas comes from a store on wheels.) The market stretches for what seemed like acres and offers more clothes than I've seen at the mall. The necessities of life are also there. You can find everything from wine making tools to baby clothes.

The town next door to Pontelandolfo, Morcone, has its market on Sunday mornings. Morcone from afar is a magical town. Its Mediterranean colored homes appear to cling to the side of the mountain. They have been clinging there for a thousand years but still amaze us every time we look up. I mention this because in order to go to the market you have to drive up and up to the town's main drag. It is the same street that houses the local medical center. Strolling the Morcone Market, I've noticed higher end vendors that don't come to Pontelandolfo. I even found one who sold fabric like luscious wools, silks, tapestries, the works.

One unfortunate day, my knee was acting quirky, and I needed to get to the health center. My steely cousin Giusy drove me there. We drove up towards that main street. What? This isn't Sunday yet the street was blocked with vendors! We didn't realize it was a special festa day in Morcone. On Festa days, people need something to do – like shop – and the vendors parade in. Giusy, being adorable and an actress, rolled down the window and smiled at the closest police officer. While she smiled even more, she explained how much pain I was in. The officer let us in! Like a contestant in an obstacle course high stakes race, Giusy steered her car in and out of those vendor trucks. She was a pro. Not one shopper was crushed. We made it safely to the health center. She dropped me off and went shopping. It was a win-win.

On a Wednesday that followed a particularly boring Tuesday, I was looking forward to watching the trucks parade in and transform Pontelandolfo's Piazza Roma into a Centro Commerciale. When I got up, I yelled down the stairs to Jack.

"Are you ready to go?"

The wind was whistling, chasing the heat from another hot summer day and dumping sand from the Sahara onto our car. How great that forceful breeze felt.

Then I bellowed, "There is laundry in the washing machine. Jack, if you're ready please hang the towels up, outside." Having a clothesline and air-dried clothes are one of the perks of living in the country. Jack came back in red faced.

"The towels will be dry in about ten minutes if the wind doesn't take them to London. It is too windy – there won't be a market."

Psshaw, I thought. Pontelandlofesi are mountain people. What's a little wind? I shoved Jack back out the door.

When we got outside the wind grabbed my hair and twirled my head around. Ouch. It tossed me towards Top Grigio.

Jack said, "There won't be a market."

"Not be a market," I screamed over the wind. "These vendors are tough, and I have to buy Zia Giusipinna a sweater for her birthday."

Jack sighed and drove us down to the piazza.

Gleefully, I shouted, "I see the trucks!"

Jack pointed out that the owners were still in the trucks and nothing was out to be sold. There were lots of cars, so people were here. Ahhh, they were sitting in their cars too.

Sadly, no one was walking around, chatting, haggling or buying. The downside of an open-air weekly market is that it is an open-air market. Sometimes the air is full of rain, wind, snow, hail or sleet. Not to worry. There will be another market next week.

Where's Midge??

Driving to our house in the Sannio Hills is a joy. Every mile, Jack and I look at each other and say, "bella vista." The mountains in the spring are alive with color. In the summer, the fields of grain turn the hills into a patchwork that any quilter would envy. We have driven to our town from different directions through a variety of hills and valleys. It really is a great ride. All of our guests have agreed – until they couldn't find us.

"Where is Pontelandolfo? Did we pass the sign?"

"Is this the turn? I can't see the signs behind the weeds."

"Maybe this is the turn off to Pontelandolfo. Get out of the car and see if you can read the name of the town under the black paint."

"Great graffiti - no rust. Does that say Pontelandolfo?"

"Watch out! Any second that dented sign can crash down on the hood."

The street signs leading to town are a wreck. When I ask the powerful people why, I get the perpetual really long sigh and look of disbelief.

"We can't fix it. It is the state."

"Of course, I would fix it but – tsk, sigh – the region."

"Midge, this is Italy – you don't understand."

We tell people we like to follow the signs to Landulphi, a now defunct restaurant. Why follow the signs to a closed restaurant? Because the street signs to the town may never be fixed. Landulphi, when it was open, put up great bright brown and yellow signs from the highway directly to the center of town. When friends come to visit for the first time they follow the Landuphi signs. I meet them in the piazza and they follow me home.

We rent a great space that is one house away from the cemetery. The cemetery is big, has huge metal gates, tombstones and crosses. What great landmark – right? Once you find the town, you can find the cemetery and our house is oh so obvious.

Then why couldn't the UPS guy or the postman or any delivery person find us? How about this factoid: our landlord's family has owned this house for generations. Jack and I always include our landlord's name in our address but still the mail never finds me. That first year the post office van zoomed right by us. Is it because I am a middle-aged woman – actually a wee bit more than middle-aged - and I'm freaking invisible?

I knew I was invisible in the United States. How many times have I been ignored alone at a bar waiting to order a drink? Enough that I had to learn to bellow: "bar keep – invisible woman here." In Pontelandolfo, not only was I invisible but our house was too. It is a big house – parts go back to the middle-ages but...

...damn, I just got it. The house goes back to the middle-ages and a middle-aged woman lives in it. Of course - we are both invisible!

A *codice fiscale*, like a social security number, is necessary to buy anything big or do any large financial transactions. Topo Grigio took me to Benevento and I registered for one. They said not to worry it would be sent to me *subito* – right away. My typical "plan for all contingencies" self had the card sent to me, in care of our landlord, at our address. Where did it end up? About a mile up the road at another family of Guerreras. That family called my cousin Carmella – whose mom is a Guerrera – and asked who Margaret Ann was? Carmella's husband, Mario, went and got the letter and delivered my mail to me. Thank God it is a small town. Our first year, the postman refused to believe that a Guerrera could live where we live because a Guerrera never lived where we live. I guess he never saw me when I said hello at the end of the driveway.

When we sold our house in New Jersey, but before we stuck those super precious can't live without them items in the ten-by-ten-foot storage unit, we sent three large boxes of stuff to Pontelandolfo. Super important stuff – like my grandmother's cast iron griddle and winter coats. The saga of the boxes is another story – but for now just know that even though the boxes were addressed to me, in care of my landlord at his address, they were delivered to my cousin's mother! Once again Mario magically lifted the cloak of invisibility from our house and guided the big truck back up the street to us. Che fa?!

I tried to call Harry Potter and see if he could conjure up some anti-invisible cream. He never answered. Maybe my calls just drift away into the land of indiscernibility?

I ordered a part for my laptop from Apple Italia. (OK, OK, I forgot the charging cable – stop laughing.) Now Apple is one of my favorite companies. They have great service and are so helpful. Since I needed the cable quickly, we arranged for it to be shipped via UPS. The driver texted me that morning – a nice touch. I replied the house was very close to the cemetery and my landlord's name was on the gate. Then I described the house and the little rented car that would be sitting out front. That afternoon, he called and said, "I can't find the house."

"Where are you?" I asked.

"By the funeral agency," he replied.

"What? I texted we were next to the cemetery."

"But where are you," he whined, "which house?"

I told him I would meet him at the cemetery – it is the only bloody one in town. After walking down to the cemetery's front gate – it took all of 3 minutes – I waited in the shade of a mausoleum.

Where is he? What – was that him?!

The truck drove right past the only person standing on the street in front of the cemetery - me. I was obviously invisible.

Rather than leave you on such a sad note, he did turn around, smile whimsically as only a twenty-something Italian hunk can and gave me my package. I sucked in my tummy, took the package and smiled back.

Can you find Pontelandolfo? I'm just curious, can **you** see me?

The Tower

It seems like every little village in the Sannio Hills has a castle. Pontelandolfo has one called Grande Bugia... okay, that is a big lie. It *had* a castle, now the only thing left of it is La Torre. The tower, surrounded by the requisite wall, has hundreds of stone steps leading up to the best view in the town. Currently, the castle property is privately owned and it is a big deal to be allowed inside the stone walls to check out the lovely garden and villa. I was so excited when I got the invitation to visit the town's logo in real life. I couldn't wait to climb the small stone steps all the way to the top. Then I did it.

I will never ever do it again!

For the young of body, getting to our tower is a cake walk. For us older beings who prefer reading to body wrenching sports, climbing the cobblestone street to the tower is torturous. I tried to drive up the vertical hill and the car starting panting and rolling backwards. When the car and I got to the top, I realized parking on a medieval hilltop is hazardous to one's body, mind and car.

Behind the gated walls there is a tranquil garden full of statues and historic monuments. A giant door at the base of the tower opens slowly. We peak inside. The first thing I notice is that the ground floor is set up as a circular bar replete with devices of torture on the walls. (Man, when the bartender flags you better just smile and leave.) The second thing I see are stone steps that are over a thousand years old and have been walked on by millions of people. They are no longer straight and flush. It would be like climbing on rocks. Not that I have ever, even in a fantasy, climbed on rocks.

Gulp, I brought this group to visit the tower and I need to smile bravely and start climbing. Worse, for me – since I was a chubby thing – the circular route up seemed to get narrower and narrower. Anxiety gripped my chest and butterflies fluttered in my belly. Goaded on by those behind me, it took me a week to crawl up to the top. Thank you, lords and ladies. I made it!

Wheeze, aaahaaa, aaaahaaaa, wheeze, I was too winded to enjoy the view. After a few minutes clinging to the tower wall and not looking down, I took a tiny step forward, looked around and panicked. Shit, it is high. If your enemies breach the walls and climb the tower a simple shove will send them plummeting to death. It was really, really far from the ground – the cars in the piazza look like tiny Tonka trucks. I would hate to be Rapunzel trapped in this place. My hair would need two hundred years to grow long enough to reach the bottom. Then it hit me – I have to go down those steps.

My heart was beating in my chest. I must have looked like I was about to pass out. The Vigile – local policeman – who came up with us asked what was wrong. Now, I was not only clinging to the wall farthest from the edge, but I was also sinking to the ground.

"È troppo alto. Ho paura dell' altezza!"

Tears rang down my face – I am the leader of the visiting group and I just admitted to being afraid of heights. So scared that I couldn't look down the steep circular stairway to death.

Il Vigile said, " Non ti preoccupare. Non ci sono problemi."

Don't worry? There is no problem? I can't move. My body became harder than the rocks that formed the tower. This dashing Vigile took my hand and guided me to the stairs – well maybe he dragged me. Then he went down two steps and stopped. Turning he put my hands on his shoulders and told me I wouldn't fall because he was guiding me down. When we got to the bottom, I kissed the ground and turned to kiss him but thought it might not be seemly. Sigh...

When I was a kid, being a princess wasn't part of my mindset. I knew I'd follow the path of my ancestors and be a serf. You would find me in front of the castle walls plucking chickens for some lord and lady's dinner. The lady, too delicate for such a chore, sitting on her velvet cushion having her hair brushed by her lady in waiting. (Man, what were those ladies waiting for anyway? The lord to cheat on his lady perhaps.) I had a fantasy of what my life was like in a castle on the hill. It wasn't pretty.

Who knew that castles were really big stone forts? Designed to keep the bad people out and the good people in. Putting them up high means you can see the marauders before they get to you.

There is some drama over who built our tower.

Some say that in 980 the land was given by the Beneventan Prince Pandolfo Capodiferro and his son Landolfo, to the Benedictine monks of Montecassino. It could have been the monks themselves who built the castle with the tower that is now painted on dishes, ashtrays and refrigerator magnets.

Why would monks need a fort to hide in?

Why would monks build a tower that was designed specifically for military use?

Why aren't the monks making wine?

Another version of our founding story and the creation of the castle is based on a piece of art. A coat of arms hidden in the village's mother church of Saint Salvatore, tells the tale of Prince Longobard, "Landolfo."

I love this version. There was this prince, Landolfo, sitting high on his horse when he came to a fast-moving stream. What is a prince to do? He built a bridge and called it Pontem Landulphi." Get it - the bridge of Landolfo – Pontelandolfo!

Once you have a bridge the evil ones could also cross it. That means it was time to build a castle. A historian noted in 1134, that a castle for some centuries dominated the territory of Pontelandolfo. *Dominated* – wow, that is heavy.

I appreciate the grace and stature of our tower but unless someone I loved was trapped by an evil gnome at the top, I will never climb it again. It stands tall over Piazza Roma and reminds us of who we weren't and who we are - strong, resilient Pontelandolfesi.

Year
Two

The First Purchase

Living in sunny Southern Italy for four months was a mere taste, a tease. The following year we decided to take the plunge and stay in Pontelandolfo for six long and glorious months. This presented a roaring car rental problem. No dealership would rent us a car for six months. Niente! Not a one. Apparently, a four-month shadowy rental is OK but six months? Nope. Is there car specific numerology? Or just a conspiracy to get the crazy American lady to buy a car?

I was scared. Buying a car would mean making a commitment to come back often or to stay forever. The rental idea is flip, hip and lets us play at commitment. Buying a car is like moving in with someone. You like the handsome honey, and the sex is great, but do you actually want to see him every day? I mean really, wash his socks, be nice to his mother and put down the toilet seat?

Jack and I each took a deep breath and said, "We will buy a car – sight unseen." We wanted it sitting in our driveway when we got to Italy. We imagined dropping the bags, jumping in our new used car and hitting the bars in Piazza Roma. Was this asking too much?

Guess who was the only dealer willing to sell us – with the cash to come later - a not quite new car sight unseen? Of course! Furbo, last year's dealer who knew we were good for the euros. It would be another little Fiat. We landed in Naples and talked about where our little old new car would take us first.

When we got to Pontelandolfo – the car wasn't there. Actually, the car we were promised wasn't available the entire first week. Living in the mountain village of Pontelandolfo is truly wonderful. I love walking down the hill daily to go to the bar for my morning coffee, staring at the piazza, writing for a few hours, staring some more, buying the day's fruits, vegetables and visiting the butcher for fresh meat. I loathe walking up the hill with three sacks of food, my purse and laptop. Where is the damn car?

Week two and we still don't have the car.

Someone whined, "We need toilet paper, bleach, dish detergent, bottled water, wine, more wine. Where is the freakin' car?"

Brrring – right on cue my phone rang.

"At the Ponte Train station?" I queried.

Our help-us-buy-a-car buddy had called, "Yes the car is ready and waiting for you at the Ponte Train Station - the keys are in it. Furbo's guy didn't have time to drive it all the way to Pontelandolfo."

"Whoa - where - what color - how will I know?"

"It is a Gray Fiat. The keys are in it. No problem, it will be easy to spot at the station."

My ever-wonderful cousin, Annarita, drove me to Ponte. When we got to the train station, we laughed so hard that her little four door Lancia was dancing in the parking lot, and I was savagely crossing my legs. Do you have any idea how many gray Fiats are parked at a busy train station on any given day? I can tell you - lots - a hell of a lot. We didn't know where to begin. Getting out of the car I walked right, to the end of the lot, and she walked left.

Feeling like Thelma and Louise, we started trying to open the doors of gray Fiats. Smart owners lock theirs.

"Hey, this one is open - no keys."

"Found another one - keys are in the ignition."

"No, he said they'd be in the side pocket."

"How about this one - reeks of pot."

"Keys in the side pocket?"

"No, in the ashtray."

"Anything else in the ashtray???"

"Hmm! Well, now that you asked, just ashes."

"Got one - this must be it. The keys are in the pocket."

"Weeeee oooo!"

I drove the car home and got a call telling me to take the cash to the dealer pronto. Cash - no credit cards this time. We bought a gray 2003 Fiat Silva for 3000 euros from Furbo and that included 6 months of car insurance! The insurance cost about 600 euros. Get this, he promised he would buy the car back after six months. Damn, we did good.

Jack and I sat in his little office. I pulled the wad of cash out of my special hiding place. Even though I then dropped a bra cup size, he took it with a smile.

"Don't you want to see my passport?" No response.

"Don't I have to sign something?" He raised an eyebrow.

"Don't I get the title to the car?"

Finally, he answered. "No. Perche? In six months, you bring it back."

"Don't I get any documents in my name?"

I got a slip of paper with a scrawled signature on it that said I gave the dude money, and he gave us a car. In the glove compartment was the insurance – in his name or maybe in the name of the guy he bought it from. He reminded me he did promise to buy the car back when we left for the USA. What a deal!

Driving home after delivering all the cash, we noticed that the air conditioning wasn't working. Air conditioning had been our absolute requirement. So, the next day Jack and I brought the car back to Furbo. He said it would take a day to fix our little old new car. I guess I looked really sad – or maybe I looked, I may stand on the desk and start screaming scary mad - so he lent us an Alfa Romeo convertible for the day.

Weeeooo super glamour. Imagine Sophia Loren and Marcello Mastroianni cruising around the countryside looking at the magic of the mountains. Jack and I were feeling like two svelte movie characters on a grand adventure. It happened to be my birthday and the joy of exploring medieval mountain villages in a sexy car, with the top down and me sporting sunglasses and a scarf sounded like the perfect gift.

Suddenly, Jack looked grim.

"Sophia, look in the car's manual. What does a rectangle with an arrow mean?"

Shit, more warning-lights came on. I grabbed the book and lost my scarf. "It means we are fucked."

The car started to buck – maybe she didn't like my cursing. *Ba Ba buck buck buck. Errrr Errr zzzzzzz ba ba buck buck.*

Double shit, Loren and Mastroianni are out in the middle of double buck nowhere joy riding. Where the buck buck are we? Jack turns the car in the general direction of the car dealer. The general direction is not downhill!

Triple shit! Why are those big black birds circling above us? Who ever said convertibles were fun?

The motor slowly fades to nothing. Have I mentioned it is my birthday? Buon compleanno a me! So much for a great day exploring the countryside. My calm husband rolled the sexy Alfa Romeo into a gas station, and I called  Furbo who is now living up to his sly and crafty name. I will say that in less than 20 minutes La Signora – that is me the scary senora - was picked up and transported back to the dealership.

They gave us a nondescript white something car. It had four tires and ran. It ran for six hours. Then it stopped running. It sweat a little and cried a little but wouldn't put one wheel in front of the other and move away from the front of the house. I called the dealer, drank two scotches and went to bed. The next morning the car was gone.

About two days later, we got great news. The air-conditioning on the first car was fixed. Yeah! All I had to do was beg a ride from someone and pick up the car. Our little old new car, now christened Silva, was not a glamour car like an Alfa Romeo but it runs and in October I get to sell it back to the dealer who I think shall now remain nameless. That means for tons less than a normal long-term rental, we have a car and we will sell it back recouping some of our cost! Yeah for us!

Imagine my joy when I discovered that here in Pontelandolfo my cousin's husband Mario had family in the auto mechanic business. I'm a Jersey girl, I know how important connections are. We brought our old new car in because the tires were practically bald, and Jack thought we needed new shock absorbers. What a surprise, over the next few months the car needed a lot of mechanical shit.

Ka-ching, Ka-ching, Ka-ching. Of course, I kept a log and all the receipts.

After six months of driving the car around town and as far as Naples, we drove back to the dealer. It was time to sell the car back. I had a list of all the money we had put into it. Particularly, I pointed out the new tires. Now, was the time to recoup some of the two thousand euro we tossed out the car window! As we drove there, I thought, *Cripes, I hope he doesn't ask for the title – since I never got one.*

Furbo, living up to his name, bought the car back for €1500 complete with its new tires, spark plugs, shock absorbers and more. He made out well. But then, maybe we did too. We spent a total of €3500 and had a car for six months. I stood there.

"Arrivederci," he said.

"No," I said raising an eyebrow and using my school administrator voice, "we paid cash. Where is my cash?"

"This is a business; I can't give you cash. I'll wire the money Senora. Don't you trust me?"

I didn't trust him, and we had a plane to catch.

"Puleeze," what do you think – of course. I pointed out again, this time in my mean queen voice, that I had given him cash and expected cash back. The Senora was pissed.

"Boh," he said looking at me like I was pazzo. "Who buys a car for cash? I will wire you the money."

The incentive to pay me may have been my Italian friends visiting the sly dealer quite a few times over a two-month period. Or maybe Furbo remembered to send the wire just before we returned to Italy and burned down the dealership. The money finally made it to my account.

Questa l'Italia!

The Quest

When you live in a part of Italy that has a bella vista at every turn in the road, any excuse for a drive on a beautiful day is a good excuse. I think my excuse on this particular day was I didn't want to hang up the laundry. My adventuresome niece, Alex, was visiting us. It is even more fun to hop in the car and explore new places when you have great company - or in this case, a "you can do it" cheerleader. The sun was shining, the clouds were floating over the rolling hilltops and there was gas in our new-old Fiat, Silva.

This crisp clear wonderful day also happened to be the second Sunday in September, the one day a year they hold a mass in Santa Maria degli Angeli, an ancient stone mini chapel in Pontelandolfo's mountains. We were in the car, deciding if we should take a left or a right out of the driveway, looked at each other and both said, "The church in the hills - *al' avventura!*" We went to find that 16th century church and - as many unplanned excursions are – it was the beginning of an incredible adventure.

Here is a little back story about the church. Many Pontelandolfesi, including my ancestors, were *contadini*, farmers and, more often than not sharecroppers, farming the mountains for a piece of the vegetable pie. Others were shepherds, alone high in the hills, minding the flocks of cows, sheep and goats. Stone *rifugi*, shelters that were little more than huts, were and still are scattered in the hills. One dark night from the doorway of a rifugio the face of a single shepherd was suddenly contorted with fear. The air around him began to twirl and spin, spin and twirl until he was sucked up into the vortex of a giant tornado. His flock of sheep whirled around him. Panicked, he did the only thing he knew might save him: he prayed to the Madonna. Pledging to build a church in her honor wherever he landed, he prayed to be put down safely. He prayed and prayed and prayed. Until *smash, boom, bang*, he hit the ground. Dazed, but committed to the Madonna, he looked around to memorize the spot. It took a few years, but he made sure that the chapel got built

That is the tale that I have been told by many of the folks in my village. Being a skeptic, I've done a little research and discovered other versions of the creation of the chapel - something about the Brotherhood, Pope Orsini, earthquakes, priests, nuns and well, stuff that Dan Brown novels are made of. However, the Wizard of Oz-esq legend suits my sense of drama.

The church was used a lot in the 17th and 18th centuries. The contadini, working and living in the mountains, made it their religious home. Times changed, and people moved on to bigger houses of worship. Now, the charming little space is only open one day a year. This was that day and Alex and I were going to find it.

Have I ever mentioned the irony of living in a southern Italian mountain village and hating roads that were based on goat and donkey trails? Narrow roads without guardrails that, like that tornado, whirl up the mountain, twisting and turning, scare the hell out of me. When Jack drives, I clutch the old lady hand-grabber, scream, moan and refuse to look at the beautiful valley hundreds of feet below that is calling me to a sure death entombed in a twisted heap of metal. The views are incredible! So, I'm told.

Was I going to admit my phobia to a young niece who has toured the world alone, decided to go to university in a foreign country and has been fearless since birth? Not on your life! All my years of working in theatre have paid off. I can put on a very brave front. Alex and I got directions to the church from my pal Nicola and started driving up a mountain. I prayed Silva would make it up the hills.

Gulp, I wasn't kidding about the whirling and twirling narrow roads. Shit, I had to keep smiling while what seemed like a donkey path was taking us up higher and higher. I couldn't even take my eyes off the road to look at the fluttering silver green leaves of the olive trees that covered the hillside. We followed the directions - I swear we did - but somehow were climbing closer to our celestial forbearers than I was super comfortable with. Little Silva started coughing. (No, please don't stall out.) I drove up in a straining first gear. Alex was the force that kept me going. Wending my way up and up to certain death by careening around a curve and off a cliff, I was scared shitless.

Alex kept saying "I feel it - we are almost there - this is right." We kept peering left - Nicola said we couldn't miss it - on the left just past the old fountain. Which old fahkackata fountain? We passed a ton of old fountains. Fountains that were divided into basins so you could do laundry. Fountains that were pipes coming out of rock. Fountains festooned with "Don't Drink This Water" signs.

"Stop the car. Stop the car!" Alex shouted. "I see horses. Maybe some people role-play *contadini* and ride their horses up here."

What a great and charming idea! Then I noticed that further up there was a line of parked cars. We must be here! Remembering that Nicola said to flip the car around and park pointed down the hill, I held my breath, closed my eyes and managed to turn around without pummeling us down the cliff. It was a veritable cliff – road, no ditch, six inches of grass and drop to your death. I thanked Silva for being the wee car that it was.

We walked up the mountain closer to the horses. Lots of people were gathering around and heading up towards a tent.

"Auntie M, you said it was a cute church," said Alex, "this looks like a revival tent."

"Maybe they put a tent up for overflow?"

Then we saw the cows - lots of cows. Big giant white cows festooned with bells were mooing and eating. Suddenly it hit us - it was a pagan cow worshipping ritual, or a country cow show and sale. Actually, it was more like a cow beauty pageant complete with an old Bob Barker Miss America MC type announcing the qualities of the candidates. The set up reminded us of a horse show. The show ring was near an announcer's platform. There were ribbons and trophies everywhere. These giant white cows, that graze in the mountains, were brushed and dressed for success. The owners, or trainers, moved them along like champions. Sadly, we were so enamored with our find that I didn't pull out my handy pad and take important notes - like who sponsored it and where the hell we were.

Alex scrambled up and sat on a fence to get closer to the action. I wandered around to feel the sense of community. This whirling road may just have landed us where that lonely shepherd had started his airborne journey. We were definitely in a grazing country. These farm families were proud of what they do, and this event seemed an opportunity for them to share in that pride.

My language skills weren't quite sufficient to ask a lot of dairy questions. I have no idea what kind of cattle were on display - white - they were big and white. It is amazing what you can find when you aren't looking! Who would imagine that high in the Sannio Hills I'd find a festival celebrating the grand bovine? (Did I just say that?) This is cow country – what better place to celebrate them? The backdrop was this incredible mountain vista. With my feet firmly planted on the ground, I took the time to enjoy the mountain views. Walking further around, I realized that we were just above a valley sprinkled with medieval villages. Wow!

We never did find that little church, but this, this was an impromptu experience I won't forget. After we watched the action for a while, cheering as loudly as everyone else, I did ask if there was an easier way down the mountain. Oh yeah, there was. We were close to Cerreto and could follow a road down to Telese and the highway. I knew that road! It was a road for sane people. Even Silva gurgled for joy.

Whew, I didn't mention to Alex how happy I was that there was an alternative route. However, I did tell her we would get to see new vistas, new cities and continue our adventure on the road.

Midge Guerrera

The Dance of the Baa Baa

Our little Silva was great for carrying me over the hill to my cousin Rossella's house. The road and Silva are about the same width, and these back country roads were all footpaths. Medieval *contrada*, threatening to fall into the valley below, cling to the sides of the hill. Some of these ancient stone clusters of homes, hanging on the hillside for dear life, are deserted. Others are still lived in, and the neighboring houses are used for animals.

My grandfather grew up in one of these precursors to the townhouse. A group of three or more of these two-story dwellings were stuck together in a row. These were not Brooklyn brownstones; the animals lived downstairs and the family upstairs. The heat from the animals helped warm the people above. Plus, you could keep an eye on them. I've often wondered about the smell.

There I was, tooling along near a cluster of these houses whose rooftops I see poking up from the side of the mountain. At eye level were cats sunning themselves on the clay roofs. I was going no faster than second gear, when I felt a wave coming at me from around the blind corner.

Suddenly, a tidal wave of sheep was roaring down on me. The shepherd and her dog were quickly moving the herd from a pasture back to the barn. She didn't see me in the wee little old new car, but her sheep did. Boy, was I glad this car was going back to Furbo! The road was narrow and I was on a cliff. The sheep had no option but to squeeze past my driver window, dance on the clay roof of the ancient house on the passenger side or leap on my hood and hop over the top of the car.

The car was so small that some of them made it in one grand jeté. The dance of the Baa Baa only lasted a nanosecond, but it was indelibly imprinted on my brain. My bag was on the back seat and I couldn't get to my phone, plus I was laughing so hard I wouldn't have been able to take a picture anyway. So, you just have to believe me. Stuff like this happens every day in the hills of Southern Italy. Actually, it has happened to me more than once.

When I sold Silva back to Furbo, he didn't notice the circle of hoof prints.

What is That?

It was a double caffeine kind of morning. With our eyes barely opened, we were making our way down to Bar Elimar for a *cappuccino doppio*. As we got to the tight S curve just before entering the village, traffic was stopped. We noticed people quickly rolling up their windows, blowing their horns and shaking their fists at something. A big something, standing on its two hind legs, drooling, teeth bared, was dashing between cars. Occasionally, unnervingly, it was reaching up to swat at a car. The claws on this thing were enormous – crazy bear claws. Our poor Silva shuddered with fear.

"Don't swipe at the tires," I screeched. "We just got them!"

I had no idea what this freaky thing was. A big weasel? A bear that is not a bear? Jack stared at it and simply said, "A wolverine."

A wolverine? Isn't that a sports team in some flyover state?

The well-read Jack explained: "The wolverine is the largest member of the weasel family with a propensity for ferocious behavior. Coupling that with strength out of proportion to its size, the hulk-like carnivore can kill prey many times larger than itself."

"Great news! Thanks, hon. Can it toss the car like Superman? How about break glass? Lock the bloody doors! Can it figure out how to open doors?"

Nobody could go anywhere. This brown, black, demonic-eyed thing kept leaping and weaving between the cars. We were all held hostage.

No need for caffeine now - I was absolutely awake.

Finally, bored with us or its rabid brain realized it needed to go off somewhere for that eternal snooze, the wolverine raced, then limped off towards the woods. Traffic moved on. Our car happily purred its way to Bar Elimar. The bar buzzed with the story of the monster. Card games stopped. Bets were placed on what it was. Someone even said, *cinghiale-orso* – wild boar gone rogue and bred with a bear!

Jack kept saying wolverine – *volverina*.

"Ghiottone?"

"Si, ghiottone sono volverina uguali."

Everyone was perplexed. So perplexed that coffee was tossed aside and grappa shot back.

When we safely got home, I googled "wolverines in Italy." Here is what I found: a PRO-Keds sneaker line, a graphic novel, a movie, a clothing line, a globally focused company and pages of tanks.

Guess what I didn't find? Mention of wolverines living in Italy. Apparently, the charming creature is currently found in only four European countries – Norway, Sweden, Finland and Russia. Maybe this gross guy just woke up one day and decided to head south. Nah...

Sorry, Jack, guess again. What was that giant thing?

GPS to Nowhere

Remember the days we plotted out our journeys using a map or atlas? I do. Moving forward, did you ever have Google maps give you play-by-play directions to somewhere, print them out and tape them to your steering wheel? I did. Now, our cell phones can lead the way almost anywhere, until they can't.

Coming back from the Naples Airport, I was a little sad because expat pals of ours were no longer laughing with us in the piazza but heading home to Ecuador. Trying to turn a quiet ride home into an adventure, I suggested we not use the highways but take the back roads. The first time we ever visited Pontelandolfo, that is how we got there. We followed pointed blue arrows – looking for those that said "Pontelandolfo." Climbing mountains, skirting past olive groves, and "wowing" at incredible vistas, we had a magical journey to the village that would enchant us.

"Let's pull off the highway and follow the blue arrows. Oh, wait, the arrows now point to nowhere and are painted over."

Jack looked at me, "Ok, but we use the GPS."

Did Jack just agree? I should have realized then that the world was about to turn upside down. Wheels squealed and we made a quick turn off the highway. Jack set the GPS app in his phone to Pontelandolfo. What good luck – we had pulled off at a spot where the great cameras in the sky could actually find us!

The blue arrow on the digital map had us going forward on a narrow lane like any other old cobblestone street. It seemed as narrow as Silva. We passed homes that were no longer homes but bombed out shells. The cobblestones disappeared and the road got narrower and narrower. Soon, after guiding us down a barely used dirt road, the maniacal GPS led us into some kind of a tunnel.

Actually, as we entered, I remarked that it looked like a World War II Quonset hut! Not that I had ever seen one up close and personal. Just in John Wayne movies. (When we got back, I did a quick Google search and found pictures of the same kind of thing we were in! These Quonset huts, made of metal, were used for barracks, prisoner of war camps, garages and just about anything else you can think of). Imagine the stories our Quonset hut could tell.

The tunnel seemed to be really tight. Jack had his headlights on and I was freaking out from claustrophobia. The sides of the tunnel were teasing the car's mirrors. Our little old new car started whimpering in fear. Shit. Where the fuck were we going?

I shouldn't have worried about where we were going because suddenly, we weren't going anywhere. Even though the GPS said there was a road – maybe it was a Roman Road and the GPS wasn't updated - the opposite end of the Quonset hut tunnel was blocked by a berm and trees. Did we just step into a World War II trap about eighty years too late? Whose trap was it? Our trap or their trap? Cripes, a few weeks earlier they found an undetonated bomb at our favorite local vineyard. Imagine what could be buried in this pile of dirt? There was no way to turn around or go forward.

My heart was beating so rapidly I thought it would fly out of my chest. Sweat was pouring down my head into my eyes. I tried to open my door. No way. The sides of the metal building now were not only touching the mirror, slowly they were grinding the mirrors into the car. Jack tried to get out on his side. No luck.

Determined to crawl out the back, I took off my seatbelt and tried to climb over the seats. Jack grabbed me and set me back down. Then I remembered there was no back way out. I started searching my purse for the little bottle of liquid valium they sell in the pharmacy.

Jack took a breath. "I'll back out."

"What! How? We can barely see what is behind us!"

"I'll use the mirrors."

"What mirrors? They have been shoved into the freakin' car."

"I'll use the rearview mirror."

"Are you kidding me?"

I tried to call for help on my cell phone. No signal. Didn't the armies put up antennae for these things?

Jack started backing up.

I started throwing up – but held it. I opened the window just in case.

Jack, slowly, kept going further and further back.

I kept lying further and further back on the seat. My eyes were closed and I was praying to everyone I knew. The GPS gods were losing and getting sent down off the mountain.

"I see light!" Jack shrieked.

"I see life!" I shrieked.

Somehow, Jack did get us out of the Quonset hut. I suggested he erase the crappy GPS program on his phone and we look for the old, rusted, painted over not blue pointed signs. The next phase of returning to a real road was turning the car around on a cow path that pitched to a valley. I have no idea how Jack did it. I had gotten out of the car and was walking back. Ostensibly to guide him backwards but frankly it was self-preservation.

After turning the car around and telling me to get back in and stop whining, Jack reminded me that it was my idea to get off the highway and take back roads. *Gulp*.

I said not a word. Just smiled and blew my brave husband a kiss. We did take a scenic route back to Pontelandolfo. It involved locating bars in every ancient village off the highway.

How Much? Don't Worry!

I have always been really afraid of being somewhere and not having enough money to pay the bill. Maybe it is because when we were little, we really didn't have enough money. In my earlier lean adult years, I would count my cash down to the penny and search the car seats for more. The thought of getting to the cash register cashless was one of those nightmares I never wanted to have, but often did. To this day, I check my purse and make sure my wallet is there. Then I check my wallet to make sure the money that was there last night is still there this morning. Then I get in the car and check to see if there is gas. Minutes before entering a store, I again open my wallet to triple check for money. Maybe it is paranoia. Maybe I'm terrified of once again tossing stuff on the supermarket belt, watching the rolling numbers in the cash register *cha-ching* higher and higher, realizing I don't have enough money and yanking things off the belt.

This ever happened to you? Did you sink down below the counter? Frantically start pulling things off the belt? Or do what I have done, drop my head down in shame and slither away?

In Pontelandolfo, where everybody knows your name, not only is that not something for me to worry about, but I have had a hard time getting people to let me pay them. Trust and sense of community are important aspects of life in our little village.

Some true examples:

Jack went to our supermarket, Gran Risparmio, and filled the cart with things we needed. He never checks to see if his wallet is there or if someone picked his pocket. Oops, maybe he should start. He went to pay and was €20 short. Did he sink below the counter? Nope, the man at the register packed up the groceries, handed them to Jack and said pay me later. When Jack told me, I was so embarrassed that I leaped into Silva and raced back to the store to pay. They were shocked to see us so soon.

Another day, I was behind an older woman in Conad, our second miniature supermarket. She was mildly confused about what she was buying, what she was cooking for *pranzo* and where her wallet was. Mariagrazia, the super nice cashier, looked at her, smiled and said, "I know you will be back and you will have your wallet then."

"Grazie cara," the woman whispered

It took all my theatre training to remain uninvolved in the story. I wanted to either pay for her or leap over the counter and kiss Mariagrazia. It was such a gentle moment and obviously one that has been repeated. My gut reaction was that someone else would be in later to settle her tab.

One night, I brought a large group to Sesto Senso, my favorite local eatery. We had a fabulous seafood meal, enjoyed bottles of wine and sipped digestivos. I walked up to the cash register with a credit card in hand. Claudio swiped it in the machine. Then he swiped it again. I started to sweat. *Shit, had I forgotten to pay the bill?* Claudio looked at me and said the machine doesn't work. It has been happening all day. Pay us next time you come. What!!!??? I made absolutely sure we went back for dinner the next night with enough cash for both bills.

The producer in me loves to toss grand parties and events. For a particularly large and whimsical week of events, I booked a number of people to work with me, ordered all kinds of food and booze, hired musicians, a theater company, caterers and more. Getting prices was difficult. Creating a budget became such a nightmare that I soon tossed it into the nightmare trash barrel. *Questa é l'Italia!* Go with the flow.

We have an exceptional bakery, Diglio Forno, I ordered a carload of stuff for a hoity toity British Tea Party. I had a great time choosing mini pastries, bizarre tiny sandwiches, scones that weren't scones and my favorite Italian pastry sfogliatelle. It was enough food to sate the twenty invited women. When I asked if he wanted a deposit, Antonio, the owner, looked at me like I was crazy.

We have a talented guy, Vittorio, who provides theatrical lighting and sound for many of the major festivals in the region. I once asked him to handle the technical aspects of two public events. Getting a price was hard but getting him to take the money during the show was even harder. He too looked at me like I was from another planet. I found out later that it often takes him months to be paid by the towns and companies that hire him. I was an anomaly. Could I get one person to instantly accept the cash I had for them in an envelope? Don't worry. Pay me later. Pay me after the show. Pay me next time I see you. Don't worry!

When I am not in town and need to send flowers for a funeral or birthday, I call Nella at her flower shop. She doesn't ask for a credit card. She doesn't tell me what it will cost. She simply creates an arrangement and delivers the flowers. When I am back, I pay her.

It isn't that folks don't want to be paid or don't feel they deserve their stipend. I believe it has to do with a real sense of community. More than community, it is a sense of family. Those of us who live here are part of the familial fabric of the village. Family who treats each other like family. I'm guessing strangers in our midst might not be extended the same courtesy.

People who provide services, own shops or restaurants know their community. They know where their clients live. *Know* is the operative word. Knowing your neighbor and knowing who you can trust. Sadly, shopkeepers tell me, that also means knowing who you can't trust.

I think one of the reasons I feel so connected to Pontelandolfo – besides the fact that I can feel my nonna here – is that the lifestyle and sense of community reminds me of Flagtown, New Jersey. Growing up in Flagtown, when the dinosaurs roamed the earth, I spent my youth knowing everyone in that village and not worrying about falling off my bike because someone would pick me up. There was the same sense of familial community that I am blessed with in Pontelandolfo.

Year Three
(and Every Year Since)

New Car Blues

"What do you mean it will take thirty days before I can pick up the car? You have a brand-new Fiat 500 L that I love parked in this showroom. I have the money in my pocket. (Well not really in my pocket but it was in my Italian bank account and a *bonifico* – wire transfer – from one Italian bank to another takes about 30 seconds on my phone.) Why can't I give you the money, you sell me that car and I drive away tomorrow?"

"We have to wait for the documents," the dealer said.

"From where?"

"Romania."

"What? Romania? This is a Fiat. Fiats are Italian cars. Why are the documents in Romania when the car is now in Italy?"

"Yes, that is correct," he said smugly, "the car is a Fiat which is an Italian manufacturer that built the car in Romania and now the car is in Italy. It takes thirty days."

What a putz, I thought. I glared, deciding he didn't want to sell the car to a woman and stormed out.

Three car dealers later – repeating the scene three times at least improved my Italian automobile vocabulary – I finally got a dealer who said it would only take three weeks – 21 days. Wow! What a well-greased business this is. I bought the car from the fourth dealer and gave him half the cost up front. When the documents got here, I would give him the rest.

Huzzah, on day 19, the dealer called and told me the documents arrived! What good news! I wired the rest of the money. Duh, why did I wire the rest of the money? I knew I made a mistake when he said, "Now the rest is easy. We just transfer the title."

On day 21 I called and asked, "When would be a good time to pick up the car?"

"Not today, the man in the office is on holiday."

"What man? What office?"

"The government office – he does the title transfer."

"Great, I will come tomorrow."

No, that is a festa day and no one works.

"Dopodomani? Day after tomorrow?"

"We will see."

"We will see. We will see!" I roared. He hung up.

Three days later, day 24, I called. "I have a ride and will come today to get the car."

"There is a problem in the government office. Giorgio is taking a longer holiday and they can't find the files."

On day 25, the dealer was now never available to take my call. His secretary - wife, I think - said he was out. I explained they had my money and I didn't have a car.

She calmly said, "Since his extended holiday, Giorgio now has much work backed up – and the title isn't ready."

"Where is Giorgio's office?" I asked.

"Why?"

"I will go there today and sit there until he does the paperwork."

"That is not a good idea. It will make it slower."

"How about I go there with €100? Would it go any faster?"

"Hmmm," she said – but still wouldn't tell me where the office was.

Day 26, I called.

Day 27, I called.

Day 28, I called.

Day 29, I called.

Day 30 – Day 30! Before I finished my morning cappuccino, the dealer called me and said he had great news! I could come now and pick up the Fiat 500 XL. *ARRRRRRRUUUUUUGGGGHHHHHHHH.*

Obviously in Southern Italy, it takes thirty days to buy a new car. Again, questa è l'Italia.

I named the Fiat 500 L Fernando – bold adventurer. Now that I waited thirty days for the car, I see a lot of adventures in our future.

" Fernando 500 "

Finding the Cavalieres

"NOOOOOO," I screamed as we rounded a tight curve and a gaggle of tourists on motor scooters aimed for us. Clutching the seat belt tighter, I pleaded with Jack to slow down.

"I'm in first gear," he said through gritted teeth.

The road we were on is famous for its S curves, beautiful view of the Mediterranean and if your car careens off the edge a million feet above the sea, instant death. It is August – tourists from everywhere love the Costiera Amalfitana.

Millions converge on those idyllic towns that make up what we all think of as the glamorous Amalfi Coast. They came to places like Positano, Ravello, Cetara, Amalfi and Praiano long before the 1997 dubbing of the strip as a UNESCO World Heritage Site. Tourists obviously love the crush of umbrellas and bronzed bodies.

"Watch where you walk," I bellowed out the window as the crowds of pedestrians added another level of danger to the narrow road.

"Is she topless?" Jack stared out the window.

"Eyes back on the road."

There are too many cars on a long and windy road. Trucks and buses actually got stuck and a line of cars had to back up. Holiday assholes on scooters weave in and out of the traffic. I kept thinking the locals must grab the cash during the season and curse the crush after the tourists are gone.

"LOOK OUT! Notice the height of the guard rail. Notice the dents in the rocky mountain wall. See the glorious sea calling us."

I hated every bloody minute we wended our way from Salerno to Amalfi. You have heard this before but: I hate heights - roads closer to the clouds then earth, roads made for donkeys not cars. It was only to help Alanna, the daughter of our dear New Jersey friends Jeff and Sue, find her Italian roots that I would drive on this *&^%&%&& highway. Did I say "hate?" That isn't a strong enough word to describe how I feel about the Amalfi Highway. Sue still owes me a bottle of single malt scotch. I almost lost an arm against the mountain wall snapping a picture of her *cognome*, family name.

When we landed in Amalfi – and I do mean *landed* - Jack realized there wasn't anywhere to park and he couldn't turn around. He literally dumped us out. Alanna and I scrambled to the curb and took a moment to stare at the sea. The water and the sky were both the bluest of blue. It was almost surreal. The main road is sea level so we began walking up into this picture perfect town that is perched at the mouth of a deep ravine at the base of Monte Cerrato. We could immediately see why tourists come to play here. I felt like I was in a movie set in a colorful village by the sea.

But we were on a quest. The goal was to find out as much as we could about Alanna's Italian roots. Her mom's surname was Cavaliere and their ancestors left Amalfi for America. We stopped the local vigile and asked how to get to *il comune*, the municipal building. The uniformed patrolman led us there. We found *l'anagrafe*, the Office of Vital Statistics. Angela, the woman in charge was absolutely amazing. When we explained we were hunting for Alanna's family, she went out of her way to help us.

Home in Connecticut, Alanna's grandfather had worked on the family tree and had lots of detail. This made Angela's hunt for information a tad bit easier. The record books that Angela shared with us were from the 1800's. Their battered covers and handwritten interiors held not only the story of each family but also gave us a peek into their life journeys. My heart was bursting as I saw Alanna touching the names of her great grandparents. The beauty of this ancient method of record keeping is that notes about the people were also written down. Alanna discovered her family included not only farmers but also a midwife.

At one moment, Angela brought us to a window and pointed at a specific point on the mountainside. "There," she said, "there is where your great grandfather lived." Whoa! Southern Italian people have hearts that are bigger than the Mediterranean Sea. Angela not only spent an hour or so with us going through the dusty records, but she discovered something unique and very personal to share.

Alanna gathered up her notes and we profusely thanked Angela for all her help. I called Jack and asked where he parked. I could hear horns honking and engines whirring.

"Parked? It was impossible to park. I kept on driving Costiera Amalfitana. Finding a place to turn around and doing it again. Go stand where I dropped you off. I'm almost there again."

Amalfi Coast! Oh shit, there is no other way back to the highway but on the same narrow death-defying road. Bam – stai zita - I think a Cavaliere just smacked me on the back of the head and told me to shut up. Alanna's ancestors walked these very streets and thought nothing of it. They drove donkey drawn carts (that don't whiz around curves) on the same death-defying road and lived to emigrate to America. I happily got in the car, hugged Jack and closed my eyes.

Travel recommendation – Amalfii Coast – Bella Vista! Buy the postcard or go in January.

Fall Migration

Fall is a great time to be in the Sannio Hills. Olive harvests, wine festivals, crisp yet balmy weather. The kind of days that our Fernando Fiat waits for, flashing its lights and begging to be driven.

Not being the kind of car owner that ignores her car, I cajoled Jack into taking a ride out towards Campobasso. We decided to take the old Roman road through the hills, much more interesting than the highway. There are stone carved mile markers that actually go back to the Romans. From up here we can see the plain below and the sparkling water of Lago di Complatarro.

Windows down, chatting idly, my nose started to twitch. "Jack, do you smell that?"

"Smell what?"

"Cows – well, actually, cow manure."

"Your nose is off. The cows are in the mountains."

"My nose is never off – you're off."

Here, the dairy cows spend a glorious summer freely roaming about in the mountains. They all wear those Swiss-looking giant bells on their collars. Wandering around up on the mountain top feels like you've been transported to the land of Heidi. Rocks jut out and up from grass covered earth. In the past as we wandered on foot over the hills, the *ting, bing, ting, bing, bing* of the bells surrounded us. The cows who wear these bells are giant white beauties. Actually, dirty white bovine whose grandeur and grace shine through. There are really big white dogs up there too. These dogs have a job to do and they do it well. They make sure nothing happens to the cows by scaring off the hikers and wolves. Daily, the farmers drive milking trucks up to the mountain and milk the cows right where they live. What service!

Wondering why I'm telling you all this? Guess what happens before the first snow hits?

The car skidded to a halt. Jack clung to the wheel and stared. There on this winding, pothole-filled road were a herd of cows, dogs and farmers marching towards us. We were going up. They were going down.

I started snapping photos on my phone. No one would believe this. We waited, waved at the farmers as they herded, with the help of the dogs, the cows around us. I wondered if the great cheese we buy in Morcone is made with their milk.

Sometimes traffic jams are magical moments.

"I told you I smelled cows."

Snow Alert

Can we talk? Sometimes life in my charming little Italian village makes me want to scream! Or if not scream, shake the powers that be until sense falls into place. It snowed. This is an anomaly here - especially in December. Some Decembers feel like fall. No one expects snow in December - maybe that is why I should have a kinder gentler feeling about...

errrrrgggg...that scream is bubbling up again.

This particular year, we knew it would snow because I received numerous alerts on Pontelandolfo 2.0, the town app. *Beeeeeep Beeeeeep* Emergency Alert. My phone was rocking and rolling all over the table with every *beeeeeep*. Horror! The sirens wailed, alerts beeped and we were warned that it might snow for three days.

"Make sure you have fuel for heat, food and something to keep you from going stir crazy."

Being from the Northeast of America where we scoff at snow, plows are out instantly and we drive in anything, I thought the alerts were a little over the top. Ooops, I was wrong.

Shush, don't tell anyone.

We had a house full of American holiday guests and plans to go out and do holiday centered stuff – then it snowed.

Day one: snow – about an inch. No one plowed or salted the local streets. OK, not a big deal. I know money is tight and we can drive over this. Downtown, no one had shoveled the sidewalks either. (Hmmm, aren't building owners responsible for that?) Not a big deal – again only an inch. Local holiday events were cancelled and even worse news, restaurants were closed. (Hey, it was only an inch but still coming down.) Glad we paid attention to the hundredth SNOW ALERT and filled the bar and fridge.

Day two: more snow – a lot more snow and we had to get my niece to the train station in Boiano. We heard the state highway was closed going west. Luckily, we had to go east. The local roads were not plowed or salted. Ice reigned supreme. We trudged to the car, swept off the snow, slowly left town and got to the highway. Now this is interesting: the highway in Campania was fairly clean and salted. The minute we crossed the regional line into the region of Molise the highway had only been given one earlier half-hearted pass with a plow. However, we didn't skid or slide because the exit ramps were clean. We got to Boiano and back and cruised our village piazza. Nope, the sidewalks still had snow and ice and the piazza hadn't been cleared. Shops were closed. I'm glad we had the necessities of life in the house: eggs, bread, pasta and wine. Have I mentioned wine? We had lots of wine.

Day three: lots more snow. I mean tons of snow. How would we get the last of our guests to their train in Benevento? Yesterday, the road was closed. First step: dig out the car. Done. Second step: dig out the top of the driveway near the unplowed road. Done. Third step: do we have to freakin' dig out the street?! The train was due late in the afternoon, and we figured we had some options.

Sleds pulled by snow sheep sounded like the best idea. It stopped snowing – that was a good sign. Before the top of my head blew off, a backhoe started ambling up our road tossing snow off the middle of the street. Note, I said backhoe and not a plow. He made a narrow path up the center of the road. We – OK not WE – Jack dug us to the center. We got in the car and wondered what we would find. Again, the state highway was pristine. The views were fabulous. We all enjoyed the diamonds glistening from the hilltop trees. The snow covered peaks ached to be skied. Since Benevento is at a much lower altitude it was an easy, snowless yet beautiful drive.

Later that afternoon when we got back to Pontelandolfo, we noted that the piazza still hadn't been cleared and the sidewalks were awful. I asked about that and found out that building owners don't have to clean in front of their buildings. So, obviously they don't. Store owners only shoveled the boots width necessary to get into their shops. Boots on skinny little people with teeny, tiny feet.

The cobblestone piazza isn't plowed, so I investigated and discovered, one can't plow on cobblestone – how about a snow blower or a shovel? I don't know the science, but couldn't they at least spread salt? I do understand not plowing local mountain roads until it absolutely stops snowing – fiscal constraints and all that. BLEH. I really don't understand but as the elders here say *questa è la nostra vita*, This is our life.

There are some things that towns in Southern Italy do well. There are other things – not so well. The snow, for instance. Well, now I know – when you get the alert make sure you have heating fuel, food and lots of booze in the house.

Jack pointed out that we did get wherever we needed to go. So: Get over it. Take a breath. Look at the snow-capped mountains and sigh at the beauty. *Questa è l'Italia!*

Following the Dancing Pastiera

Buona Pasqua! Happy Easter! The happy salutations can be heard in every little contrada. This is the time of year neighbors visit neighbors and friends.

Cars are racing throughout the village. *Wizzzzzz* there goes a pastiera!

Vroom – watch out! Another pastiera is zapping by barely remaining on the front seat of that Lancia.

Screeeeeech – quick stop by that Volkswagen Polo and one pastiera down!

EEEEEKS – is that a flying pizza piena?

"Wait a minute – is that the pastiera I gave you yesterday? It just landed back on my table!"

My best buddy, Rossella, and I were laughing madly. The laughter was so loud that it crossed the Atlantic Ocean. As a matter of fact, the ocean must have been rockin' and rollin'. She had been telling me that she had made a number of *pastiera* – a

Neapolitan tart made with cooked wheat berries, eggs, ricotta cheese, flavored with orange flower water and candied citrus.

In our part of Southern Italy, for Easter, we practice the Neapolitan tradition of baking *pastiera* and/or *pizza piena* — crust topped pie or calzone shaped pasta stuffed with ricotta cheese and dried meats. Women from Pontelandolfo, Casalduni and other villages in the Sannio Hills visit their friends and bring them a gift of a lovingly baked pastiera or pizza piena.

As Rossella was talking, I was thinking of my Aunt Julie making "pizza chiena" in my grandmother's kitchen. She tossed in eggs, ricotta, baloney (which is nothing like mortadella), salami, capicola and rice to make a pie that would sink the Titanic. But boy were they good.

BOING – it suddenly hit me why she made three or four but we only got to eat one! She too probably took them to other people's houses. But in Flagtown, NJ there weren't any other Pontelandolfese to bring us a scrumptious gift of a homemade pastry. Boy, we lost out on that one.

Suddenly, I saw a parade of pastiera moving slowly up curvy mountain roads, into valleys, around centro storico, pausing for a moment at a house and dashing out again.

"Rossella," I said, "let me get this right. I make a bunch of pies and I bring them to a bunch of friends."

"Si, and they make a bunch of pies and bring them to a bunch of friends."

"What happens if a woman gets more pies than she made? You know, Maria brought her a pie but she doesn't have one to give Maria?"

"Hmm that could be a problem. But she could make a pie tonight and take it to Maria tomorrow.

"Or," I said mischievously, "She could give Maria the pie I made or you made. I mean, that's what I would do."

"Nooo! No one would do that – would they?"

"I bet they do. How long do you think it would take before we got one of our own pies back as a gift?"

"I am going to put a red dot on the bottom of the tin pan and see if it comes back."

"Good, I'll put a yellow dot on mine. Whoever gets their pan back buys the other an Aperol Spritz at the bar."

She started to giggle, I started to giggle. The laughter started to roll. We both got to work making our pastries.

Buona Pasqua!

Ticket?
What Ticket?

Son of a &*^%(!

ONCE AGAIN our Fiat 500 L got a ticket. Notice, I said the car got the ticket – not my *Indy 500 wanna be* speed demon husband. Tickets are mailed to you two or three months after you zoom by an autovelox. Traffic cameras, *autovelox*, – which are everywhere – clock your speed and grab your license plate number. The autovelox, however, are not sneaky, smarmy hidden in a tree camera. These are blatant speed traps. There are huge signs announcing them and most GPS devices have them listed. Ticket Giving Machine Coming Up!

If you are zooming along and suddenly all the cars in front of you slam on their brakes, slam on yours. All locals know where the autovelox cameras are and slam on the brakes to drive 5-10 miles below the posted speed. The slowdown lasts for a few hundred feet beyond the autovelox and then *zoooooooom* the cars race off again. Since Italians always slow down for these camera boxes, drive like an Italian. Jack now has an Italian passport, so you'd think he'd get with the program.

There is this great reality TV-esq game called "Speed Limit Today, Gone Tomorrow." The speed on the local roads changes randomly. *Sta attento*! Pay attention to the signs! We noticed that where the roads need repairs – and there are a lot of roads in a lot of places - the town, region or province merely lowers the speed limit on that road.

Whoops, we've got a giant pothole – *let's just lower the speed limit and go for a coffee*. The road washed away in the last flood, *let's put up some orange plastic tape to narrow it down to one lane and reduce the speed limit*. The speed limits are sometimes posted and sometimes not, so don't drive and daydream about lunch.

Now, when the latest ticket was delivered with a smile by the mailman, I raced outside and put Fernando in a time out corner. I still don't know where our car was out by itself speeding or who was along for the joy ride. Fernando Fiat 500 L would not rat out anyone.

Obviously, no one in my family would speed on an Italian road. Or not see the SIGN.

Controllo Elettronico
Della Velocità

The tickets come in the mail and we pay the fine at the *ufficio postale*. The Post Office is a fun place to do nothing. Couches and comfy chairs are set up along one wall. One can chat with friends while one waits, waits, and waits to be served. Some people just take a snooze until it is their turn. I think only one person is ever working at the counter and the local post office is a bank, store, place to pay bills, place to pay money owed to towns and, if you are insane, you can buy stamps.

Bottom line: don't get a speeding ticket and have to spend the morning at the ufficio postale!

This ticket was the third one we have been surprised to get. The tickets go to the car – that is to the person to whom the car is registered. The car is in my name. *Hmmmmmmmmmm.*

Fernando whimpered, and I let him/her out of time out. Since I don't want my insurance to become so astronomical that I can't afford to go out to dinner, I will continue in my role as the extraordinary car nag. My nagging is always done with love. *Growwwwwllll.*

Curbside Service Pontelandolfo Style

Remember those car hop joints of the 50s and 60s? We would drive up, someone super cute would come up to the car, take our order, flirt a little and come back out with little trays that fit on the car window. In Pontelandolfo, I discovered personalized curbside service with a twist.

You have probably shown up at your pharmacy's drive-up window and been handed your meds, a Covid Test swab or even a chocolate bar. Fernando and I have had a much more interesting type of curbside service at the village's pharmacy.

There aren't many things I'm afraid of. Needles, however, turn my tummy to jelly, make my teeth clench and my hands sweat. Imagine the wave of fear that washed over me when after breaking my ankle, the orthopedic doctor in Alghero, Sardegna said, "Every day for thirty days you have to give yourself a needle in the stomach."

I screamed *NO*.

The nurse said, "No? Then you die from a blood clot."

Oh, I mused, *die or get a needle in the stomach every day for thirty days?* Thirty days was the length of time I was to wear the cast/boot on my broken ankle and repose. "Gulp, I'll take the needle, but I can't give it to myself."

The nurse showed my loving husband Jack how to jab a needle in my gut. Jack did it – I think happily and with a malicious grin – for three weeks. Then he left for Venice. Cazzo, now what do I do? No way I can shoot myself up with blood thinners – *eeeeeuuuuuchh*.

Curbside Service at La Farmacia! Annarita, my resourceful personal assistant, brought me to Pontelandolfo's pharmacy.

Since I wasn't supposed to put pressure on my foot and wasn't about to hop on cobblestones, I couldn't get out of the car. Dottoressa Tina raced to the rescue! Pharmacists here can and will give needles – even if that means watching me tremble in my car.

Tina opened Fernando's door, I pulled my dress over my head, pulled down my panties and closed my eyes. Then: "Hey, did you give me the shot?"

She had, and I hadn't felt a thing.

"Wait a second, when Jack jabs me it hurts like hell. Did you really give me the shot?"

She laughed and trotted back inside. We went to the pharmacy for the entire week that Jack was gone, and I almost happily got my daily needle.

Curbside service didn't just happen at the pharmacy. Small town life is wonderful. During my wheelchair days – no, crutches and I couldn't get along - shop owners helped me, laughed with me and made sure I kept rolling along and off my ankle.

Curbside Service at La Ferramenta! I had a new sink installed and needed to buy a faucet. No way could I handle the uneven street with my hop-along walker or expect Annarita to push my sorry butt on the cobblestones. Nicola, the owner of our local hardware store, sent out to Fernando a variety of selections for me to choose from.

"And here in my right hand I have a divine stainless-steel model."

It was attractively priced and happy to sit in the back seat of Fernando Fiat. The entire transaction happened at the car.

Curbside Service at Da Tiziana! Since I was now sleeping in the dining room and folks kept stopping by to visit and stare at my broken ankle, I needed nightgowns that weren't tattered and stained. Off we went to our local clothing shop. The owner, Tiziana, dashed out with nightgowns. The curbside fashion show had us all laughing and attracted the folks strolling by.

After I decided which would suit my new princess reclining status, we realized I had to try them on. Fernando didn't shudder while I held on to the car with one hand and balanced on one foot. Then, right there in the street, Tiziana and Annarita dressed me in an interesting variety of evening wear. Psshaw! Of course, I did that over my clothes! My mamma taught me not to stand naked in the street. We visited this shop a few times to buy knee socks and other stuff.

Fernando– who by the way felt incredibly special – truly enjoyed parking his/her butt and having everyone come to him/her.

On the Roads of Apuglia

These wheels should be turning further south, whined Fernando Fiat. *Why stay parked in front of some old stone chilly house in the mountains when the sun shines brighter in Apuglia?* Finally, after our frisky Fernando kept sputtering and crackling, *Explore Apuglia* (Puglia), we agreed.

Leaving Campania and driving south through Puglia, my face pressed to the windows looking for *trulli,* those round stone huts with conical roofs, all I see on this highway are towering windmills. Windmills like a blight – I see fields of fugly windmills. There are so many on SS55 that I thought I was on the New Jersey Turnpike in the middle of an industrial zone. I know, I know windmills are good for the farmer – he gets paid rent for the land. They are good for the planet. Question: do tourists want to see fugly or interesting? The more I read, it seems like the millions of windmills in Southern Italy are really only good for the banks who have the notes, the businessmen who get the cash from the EU and of course the mob.

We just want to find the trulli! Fernando Fiat 500 L, sensing my discontent, starts driving even faster down the highway. I take my nose off the window and start scanning the atlas that is open on my lap.

Ostuni

I saw that Ostuni was just a short hop off the highway. Our empty tummies told us it was time for pranzo, so I convinced Jack to leave the highway and head for the town billed as "The White City." I had read that, contrasted with the blue of the sea, Ostuni's whiteness dazzles the senses. At this point we were starving and looking forward to dazzling our senses in a sea view restaurant perched on the hill.

From the bottom of the hill, the postcard-perfect Ostuni is indeed glittering white and wonderful to see. It literally sparkles in the noon day sun – what visual magic.

"Here it comes," you're thinking, "she is going to hit us with something not so nice."

Moi? You know, one cannot judge a book by its cover or a town by a view from afar.

As Jack cursed Ostuni's narrower than narrow streets and I stuck my head out the window looking for a restaurant, the small child in me whispered, "Momma, can we paint our house red?" No kid, you can't. Because this is the White City and the tourists would be pissed. Up close and personal, all that white on white on white was BORING.

The only splashes of color in the town came from bright laundry fluttering in the breeze. If I lived there, I would only own the brightest of colors. My orange sheets would flutter from the line. I wonder if all that white makes people sterile. Suddenly, Jack – still searching the city for a restaurant – slammed on the brakes. I looked up and saw that the teeny tiny street was blocked by a car driven and parked by a young woman. She was obviously waiting for someone – I'm thinking her nonna or an invalid.

I say that dripping with sarcasm because we waited a good 5 minutes – never honking the horn, cause we're nice. Suddenly, a door popped open and a sweet young thing dashed out – her skirt so short I couldn't figure out how she could sit without... well, never mind. She waved a *thanks* to us and hopped in the car.

UGGGGGG, now I'm really not liking this town.

We couldn't find a place to eat. We couldn't find a place to park. We were becoming color-blind. The whiteness of it all was – well – just too white. Fernando, being a black Fiat 500 L, felt incredibly off place. We left and decided to take our chances with a colorful tourist eatery on the gray highway.

La Città Di Bari

Bari is a city with thousands of year-old history and modern traffic issues. As we hoofed it around the interesting city, Fernando Fiat 500 L was sadly left behind. Our personal tour guide of the historic center of Bari was one of Puglia's biggest advocates. Salvatore made sure we walked the smallest of cobblestone streets, saw and heard the women making the orecchiette pasta they are famous for and learned to love his city.

The following information should not be shared with small children. We visited the cathedral, Basilica San Nicola. This cathedral was consecrated in 1197! We saw the tomb of Saint Nicolas. *Shhhh*. That is a secret.

Walking through the neighborhoods we heard what Salvatore calls the "WhatsApp" of the streets. Apartment houses built in squares around small courtyards came alive with conversations bellowed from balcony to balcony. Young men shouted up to their Nonnas what fish had come into the port.

"Grandma, today the sea urchin and octopus look great! Should I buy it?"

In the robo world of cellular everything, verbal banter is no longer heard. Here in the center of Bari, we still find the verbal instant messaging of a medieval village.

Bari is a modern city with an opera company, professional theater, high-end designer retailers, universities, bookstores, public transportation, and all the accoutrements that make a city a wonderful place to live. Coupled with that, one finds villages like open air markets, fishermen selling the day's catch on the pier, promenades along the sea and the medieval historic center.

What you don't find is us driving a car there.

Sammichele di Bari

Fernando was lonely, so we started him/her up and went

to find a Puglian foodie paradise – Sammichele di Bari. When we got near the small city our mouths started to salivate, our noses twitched and our stomachs rumbled. This remarkable place has more butchers per square mile than one can imagine! The butchers all have outdoor tables and roast their meats to mouth-watering perfection. As you get within the city walls, you start to smell the nightly roasting. The night we went to Sammichele, the church was holding a procession. The Saint was carried through streets magically lit with twinkling lights in fairy-like configurations.

Sorry, Fernando - one must walk into the village center - or run over people sitting at outdoor tables enjoying *zampina*. Zampina are the thin sausages rolled into a tight coil reminiscent of a small paw. The combination of pork, beef and red wine give these sausages grilled on wood fires a unique flavor. For a scant €35 a couple at Macelleria Braceria da Gerado, we indulged in mint flavored fresh peas, rosemary roasted potatoes, fava beans covered in shaved Parmesan, local olives, zampina, another meat dish that of course my addled brain forgot the name of, great bread, wine, water and - Basta.

Burp, time to roll down the street and find our car.

Kids and Cars

Everyone out there who is as old as I am can remember the fun-filled roll around in the back seat time before mandatory seat belt laws. (Clean it up! I'm talking about being a kid and not buckling into your assigned third of the seat.) As toddlers we would stand on the back seat of the car peering out the back window, sticking our tongues out at the drivers behind us. Or hanging out the side window and giving trucks the arm pull-down signal for tooting their big horns – then getting yelled out for sticking our heads out the window.

As a kid, I remember having fun-filled times riding in the back of the pick-up truck. Sitting on the edge of the truck bed and balancing as the wind whipped my face. Then there was the piece of plywood my father had cut to fit the back seat of the car that my mom tossed pillows on. It was an instant bed for long drives. So what if the car flipped and we flopped around. Somehow, we all survived and made it to – well, whatever age we are.

Then someone started keeping data on folks killed in cars. Seems a lot of people have died and many because kids like us weren't buckled in. Safety first! Seat belts save lives! Well, where car safety is concerned. Here in Southern Italy it is kind of like 1955.

Driving around Puglia, I saw toddlers standing on front seats – *wheeee* – you can really see out the window. Now, not all parents do that – I have seen kids buckled up for safety. Frankly, I see more standing on seats and hardly ever see a car seat. The child safety seats are someone lovingly holding the wee ones on an adult lap.

Why not take all three kids to school squished on your Vespa *motorini*? This one dad had a wee one standing in front of him and two squished together behind him.

The absolute worst thing I saw in Puglia was a helmetless tiny tyke on the back of a giant motorcycle clutching dad's shirt as they roared through town. Jack pointed out the kid was smiling, and I was the only one having a hissy-fit. Apparently, according to Jack, I am often the only one having a hissy-fit.

Is this car riding freedom a good thing or a not so good thing? Fernando honks, *you decide*.

Yeah! I see Trulli!

Fifteen minutes outside of Bari on our way to Nardò, Puglia I swear I saw an old stone trullo in a field. I shrieked STOP and Jack floored it. On SS 16 between the sea and the highway there is a field of Trullo just before Monopoli. Of course, we were on a highway and there were cars behind us but hey, I want to see a trullo. Sometime later I saw a sign "Trulli di Alberobello." I begged, I pleaded but NOOOOOOOO. The driver wanted to get to Nardo and unpack the apparently over tired car. On the way back, he said. I sulked.

So what is all my fussing about, you're wondering?

A trullo is a round stone hut - dating back to the 16th century - that was usually built in a field by a farmer. The area is full of rocks. It made sense to clear the field and build yourself a circular stone home. This style of construction is apparently specific to the Itria Valley of Puglia (Hmm, that must be where we are). I read somewhere that trulli could be taken down as fast as they went up. Contadini lived in them - sometimes a small collection of trulli would be built for a number of farm families. I was jonesing for the chance to see one - not the cute touristy restored ones but the kind people who lived off the land actually used.

Fernando, knowing I was insane for a trulli sighting, gave a signal to the GPS and we got lost on our way to Alberobello. Lost in the reality of farms, fields and trulli. No one saw me hop out of the car and traipse through a field interspersed with ancient olive trees. The twisted mask-like trunks and pointed limbs beckoned me to investigate an ancient trullo. It was pretty far off the road, sitting there alone and waiting for someone. (That someone was me.) Jack stayed by the car with his hand on the phone ready to call for help if the ancient rocks heaved their last sigh and fell on me. I knew they wouldn't. This dry-stone construction has lasted years and will last until someone takes it down.

As I was hiking out to the hut, I remembered that there was a scandalous theory about the construction design. No one likes paying taxes – especially Italians. Since the taxes were so high on property, people kept their eyes out for the taxman and knocked their trullo down before the taxman made it out to add it to the list. What house? *We don't have a house. All those pots and blankets piled over there? Haven't a clue who they belong to.*

Whew, I needed to breathe and sat for a bit on a large rock. I bet this stone hut was really constructed as a temporary field shelter or a place for farm workers to live. Inside it was about as big as a Fiat 500L. Hmm, smell the sheep? It was dark and damp but also cool on this hot summer day. The circular interior didn't feel cramped. Imagine mamma cooking over the fire and pappa sitting after a day in the fields. Sigh. Time to walk back and hop in the car.

Somehow, we found our way to the town of Alberobello. The town is in the province of Bari, where whole districts contain dense concentrations of trulli. On our way into town – think the suburbs of Alberobello -we saw trulli fitted out with dish antennae and utility wires. People actually still live in them. These were bigger than the one I found in the field and looked like they had been fashioned out of what had originally been a cluster of huts.

We were excited to visit Alberobello because it is such a unique place to visit and it is one of Puglia's two UNESCO World Heritage Sites. That means it is full of tourists and everything is just too, too perfect. So perfect. Each conic home was more beautiful than the next. I expected any minute to see a trullo sporting McDonald's arches. (Hey, when I was in Stratford-upon-Avon, Shakespeare's daughter's house was a Wimpy restaurant.) Alberobello was a little too "bello" for me - think Disney plastic. Time to get back in the car.

Jack and I truly love Southern Italy. Puglia is one of our favorite vacation regions. If I tell you how exquisite it is, you may all want to go there. If you go, like Venice or Florence, it may become overrun by backpack carrying tourists.

So, swear to me, even if you love what I had to say and are chomping at the bit to race there: You. Won't. Go! Come on, swear it!

Milano Here We Come

Jack and I are art junkies. One day, jonesing for an art fix, we looked at each other and said Milano! Milano is home to countess museums, designers, fashion and scrumptious restaurants. Don't tell anyone, but we like Milano better than Rome. We tossed clothes in suitcases, called our favorite B&B for a reservation and hopped in Fernando.

Woooo Hooooo! What silly kids we are! Instant adventure!

Driving along, we passed through mountains, plains, saw the ocean and paid a fortune in tolls and gas.

Along the autostrada in the region of Emilia-Romagna there were acres and acres of growing and drying herbs. It was quite beautiful until I remembered that people ingested them. Poured the herbs into their stew. Mixed the herbs with hot water and drank them. *Euccch*!! Acres of herbs and other crops getting a 24-hour dosing of global warming causing carbon monoxide emissions. Double *euuccccchhh*!

A little back story – My grandmother and Aunt Cat were the queen and princess of subsistence farmers. They used the skills they brought with them from Pontelandolfo to create a Flagtown, NJ farm chock full of good eating. No one used pesticides – who could afford them and if they killed bugs they would probably kill us. Fertilizer? Mary the horse gave you that. No disgusting crap was sprayed on the lawns to kill the dandelions. We learned to pick the young dandelions and thank mother nature for the free salad. Today, my nonna would think people spending money to make their lawns fake green and without dandelion weeds – free salad – pazzo.

"Jack, pull over – I want to see if there is a sign with the name of the company planting the herbs."

"Are you insane? We are on the autostrada, I can't pull over."

"Come on," I whined, "I need to read who sells these dried spices and herbal teas. I will refuse to buy them."

"Why," he said, "they're fine."

Determined to let him know that the spices were not "fine," instead of watching the scenery float by I stared at my phone. Aha, my Google search of the effect of carbon monoxide on plants yielded great stuff written by super smart folks – I didn't understand a word of it. I mean, neurotransmitter, regulator of sinusoidal tone, inhibitor of platelet aggregation and suppressor of acute hypertensive response, and most of above effects are...

What the @#%#? Who writes this stuff and since it was from a USA government website, who was supposed to read it?

I remind Jack that Zia Vittoria would not let me pick the wild fennel along the sides of roads – because of the cars. My grandmother wouldn't let us pick wild asparagus or strawberries close to the road either. My elders and inherently natural foodies knew the yuck from passing cars was poison. POISON!!!! Who wants to eat food covered in exhaust stuff?

Jack shook his head and reminded me that those were the same women who said you can't go outside – even in the summer- with wet hair.

Errrrrrrrggggggg. I had nothing left to say. The road to Milano was long and quiet.

Irregular Regulars

Baci, baci! Grand abbraccio! Kiss, kiss, big hugs. Within half an hour after arriving in Milano, Jack and I were embraced by Milanese warmth and passion.

We rang the bell at Il Girasole High Quality Inn's portone (humongous door protecting castles from the Visigoths) and spoke into the squawk box.

Even before the massive door was fully opened, "Midge, Jack, Bentornati!" rang out. Nicola, one of the vivacious owners squeezed through a crack between the doors and swooped me into a hug. Whenever we come to Milano – which is about once a year – we stay at Il Girasole. Co-owner Matteo came out, saw us, and bellowed "Bentornati!" Baci, baci, grande abbraccio. Big hugs and kisses to both of us.

After we got Fernando parked and we unpacked we headed up the street and around the corner to Tony's, an inexpensive restaurant that serves pretty good fish and just about anything else you would find in a great cheap local place. We walked in, asked for a table for two, took off our coats and *whomp* – heard, "Bentornati!" The waiter looked at us and said –"New Jersey right? Glad you're back – but you always come back!"

Wow – I must look like someone famous! In high school I could pass for Sally Fields in her flying nun phase and once in an airport Jack was confused for British actor, Tom Wilkinson. Maybe we give off a famous person aura?

Baaammm – then it hit me. We are irregular regulars! There is no schedule. No one knows when we will return to Quartiere Villa San Giovanni, this friendly Milanese neighborhood. But we always do. We are absolutely irregular regulars!

An Accidental Visit to Basilica di Sant'Ambrogio

The sun was shining, the air was clear, Fernando was playing nicely with a Mini Cooper in our hotel's parking lot and we were energized to take the Metropolitana to the Duomo. Every time we come to Milano, like tourist lemmings we head for the Piazza Duomo, gawk at the Gothic marvel constructed of pink veined white marble and enjoy the energy of the crowd. We've seen everything from hip-hop dancers to classical violinists busking by the Duomo.

The outside of this immense cathedral is amazing. The

facade features more than 3,200 statues. We have stared and created narratives to go with some of them. Today, we were determined to see the inside of this incredible house of worship.

There was only one problem. I run from hordes of tourists. Backpacks attack me and then I say mean and ugly things to their owners. Lines that go on forever are not enticing. Now, we knew it might be crowded. It was, after all, a glorious weekday but we had no idea...

First clue: the armed guards at every door.

Second clue: long lines waiting to get into the church.

"Vorrei partecipare alla prossima messa. Quando ci sarà?" I asked in my best adult lady voice.

The guard put his hand on his gun and looked at me. Obviously, I wasn't the first person who asked if they could go inside for the next mass. I hung my head in penance. We went to the back of the line and discovered that to go inside the Duomo you had to buy a ticket. Ok. Ok. We can do that. Hmm, where the hell is the ticket booth?

We wandered around the gigantic exterior and across a side street, finally saw the ticket and Duomo souvenirs store. Upon entering I was handed a number – 40. I was number 40 in the *lunghissima* queue to buy a ticket to stand in a two-hour line to wander with a horde in the Duomo. NOT!

I remembered reading about the quality of art and architecture of Basilica di Sant'Ambrogio, so I pulled out my map and dragged Jack in that direction. Boy, am I glad I did! It wasn't a short walk but it got us out of the tourist crunch and into a neighborhood.

Tired of walking and ready for wine and sustenance, we happened upon Caffè della Pusterla (Via Edmondo de Amicis 22). Yummy, friendly and full of local folks who were happy to help us on our journey to Sant'Ambrogio. We both had *Stinco e Patate* – pork shin - think ham hock braised to perfection and served with lemon roasted potatoes. I flashed back to my grandmother's Sunday dinners. *Ahhhh*.

After a great meal, wine and the local digestivo – Fernet –

we set off to the Basilica. Coming upon the complex, I felt like I was stepping back centuries. Saint Ambrose (*Sant'Ambrogio*) is the patron saint of Milan and was the driving force behind getting the building done. The church, originally built between 379-386 A.D., is a great example of Romanesque Style.

Today, the Basilica of Saint Ambrose's crypt is the final resting place of the patron saint. It is below the main church, in an area called the *Tesoro di Sant'Ambrogio*. Numerous martyrs from Roman times have also been buried there. Did you ever wonder how all those martyrs made it to the same city?

For €2 each, we headed down to the Tesoro to see the Basilica's artifacts. We walked through the iron gate, got our tickets and slowly walked through the exhibit of gold and silver artifacts and other objects of high artistic and religious value from the 13th to 19th centuries. The works of art that had the greatest impact on me were not made of gold, silver, silk or jewels but of found objects, scraps of cloth and stolen pieces of wood.

In 1944, Italian soldiers who were held at Wietzendorf, a German concentration camp, created a nativity scene. Determined not to compromise on their religion, these brave men created a crèche. Imagine in fear of the German soldiers, crafting something so special with just a hidden Boy Scout knife, small pair of scissors and door hinge as a hammer. We joined another couple staring at the installation and soon tears were sliding down all our cheeks.

Leave Piazza Duomo behind and visit the Basilica di Sant'Ambrogio located at Piazza Sant'Ambrogio 15. You don't need a ticket and there aren't any lines. All you will find is a pleasant opportunity to explore a historic venue in a great neighborhood.

Looking for George Clooney

Everybody knows that the casino called Bellagio in Las Vegas was named after the fabulous little peninsula city in Lake Como. You knew that right? (Admission – I don't think I knew that! Boy, did I feel stupid!) Now, I know that George Clooney hung out in a place called Bellagio on Lago Como, but I just never put George Clooney, Lago Como and Italy's Bellagio together with roulette and blackjack. Duh!

We hitched a ride with an acquaintance and headed for Bellagio. The mountains surrounding Milan were absolutely lush and green. The ride and the view were travelogue material. It seemed like only moments of breathtaking views before we were off the highway and following a long and winding road that hugged the lake. Now, I have a real aversion to curvy, narrow, guard rail-less roads that Italian drivers race along. Copycat Jack races along those horrific mountain trails, while I look out the window at impending death by impalement in rocky valleys.

Unlike Jack, our friend was a smart and cautious driver. Also, driving on this curvy narrow road, if you careened off the edge you hit water. I am a fairly good swimmer and not afraid of the water. Therefore, my knuckles weren't too white and I could enjoy the scenery. It was gorgeous! Not just gorgeous – breathtaking.

We enjoyed looking at the lake and interesting houses along the road. We parked in Bellagio at I Giardini Di Villa Melzi and met Aurelia. She was a wealth of information about the gardens – including a note about how even the numerous fireplaces can't sufficiently heat the villa and it is freezing. The villa was designed by architect Giocondo Albertolli and built between 1808 and 1810. Napoleon's pal, Francesco Melzi d'Eril was the first owner. He also happened to be the Vice-president of Napoleon's Italian Republic.

The lush park-like grounds are open to the public and worth visiting. There is a small fee but to walk back in time, stroll along the lake and take in the sculptures is absolutely worth the fee. During our stroll, Aurelia pointed out interesting architectural details and answered all my questions. There was an Asian inspired water-garden and interesting little buildings. The villa itself is still privately owned – boy, to be a fly on the wall there. Some of the guests included Franz Lizst and, of course, oodles of politicians. We thanked Aurelia for

introducing us to the garden and its history. Next time, we will bring a book, find a bench, read, stare at the lake and imagine life in the 1800s.

Jack and I went off on our own to explore the village of Bellagio. Groups of tourists were milling about the narrow streets peering in the windows.

Actually, the place was packed with tourists.

"Cripes – watch your bloody backpack! I just got smacked," I yelled.

We climbed. The streets all led up from the water. We scrambled and peered in expensive shop windows.

The place is beautiful to look at but reminded me of any of a number of places around the world that have lost the local charm of the butcher, baker and candlestick maker to shops that sell expensive touristy stuff. It was lovely to sit by the water and stare at Lago Como.

"George Clooney – in the boat," I screamed at the top of my lungs. Then laughed wickedly as the backpackers rammed into each other trying to take a peak.

Jack rolled his eyes and we got up. We then strolled to the pier and hopped the traghetto between Bellagio and Varenna. The short but wonderful ferry ride across the lake cost us €9.20 for two tickets. The next leg of the journey was a train ride between Varenna and Milano – those tickets were €6.70 each. It was great to cruise along and watch the scenery change as we headed out of the country and into the city.

Diva Does La Scala

Everyone has a fantasy right? (Not that kind!) The kind where we see ourselves, as Walter Mitty did, the conqueror of all things. I was going to be an actress who really wanted to be a cabaret singer with a dirty ditty or two. Life has been an interesting journey and some of the roads had me on stage, on film and singing a dirty ditty or two. Midge Mitty, long lost daughter of Walter, really wanted to be in the Opera! I wanted to sing on the really big stage. Now my voice would never get me there but wow, what a fantasy.

I think it's really the costumes I want – imagine those head dresses!

We were in Milan and I decided that my fantasy needed a stage - a BIG stage - Teatro alla Scala. The day before, I went to the ticket booth to see if we could get tickets. It didn't matter what we saw – I just wanted to get inside the place and absorb the centuries of music.

It's my fantasy, of course I wanted to sit in the orchestra, wearing pearls and hoping the paparazzi snap my photo.

"€250 a ticket? What? OK, how about the next ring?"

"Mi dispiace signora, we are sold out?"

No, No, I will not even be sitting up there with the

Gods. Saddened by my poor planning – yes, of course, you can buy tickets online. Yes, of course, we could have bought them months before.

I tearfully departed, stopped and started dancing in the street. We would still get in! I would still absorb the magic of La Scala and it would only cost us €5 or less – thank you for those biglietti per i cittadini anziani – by visiting the museum.

The next day we headed back to Via Filodrammatici, 2. Catchy street name – notice that *drammatici.* (Wordreference says it means exaggerated, dramatic, theatrical!) Great place for Teatro La Scala.

The 2,800 seat house opened on August 3, 1778 as New Royal-Ducal Theatre alla Scala. If those walls could only talk…

We wended our way to the iconic structure at lunch time. Teatro alla Scala Museum is located on Largo Ghiringhelli, Piazza Scala. It is essentially the side of the theater. Piazza Scala also sports for the well-heeled music aficionado, Ristorante Teatro alla Scalo il Marchesino. The celebrated Italian chef, Gultiero Marchesi creates meals that are delicious and incredible to look at. The two well-dressed men sitting next to us ordered something that was actually coated in REAL gold! They knew no one would believe them and this dapper Dan actually took out his phone and snapped a photo. We were too busy tasting and staring, staring and tasting to snap any photos. (Oh yeah, the menu was on iPads! The head waiter presents each diner with an iPad!) A wonderful experience, of course for what we spent on lunch we could have bought one of those tickets for that night's performance.

Smiling like a well fed and wine paired diva, I strolled to the museum and enjoyed every bloody minute. From peering into the grand auditorium, sitting in a box and waving at my fans, to wishing I could just wear the antique costumes for a nano second, the museum was captivating.

Castello Sforzesco

Milano really is an art lover's mecca. Jack and I didn't know where to start. So many choices! Deciding which museum to go to was like looking at a dinner menu – too many choices. "Just make me a hamburger."

We started with the exhibitions at Castello Sforzesco. Castles are cool! I love to imagine how those noble folks lived – my family would of course be serving them. When I visit a castle I become *la principessa*! Castello Sforzesco was originally built in the 14th century and then redone in the 15th century by the Duke of Milan, Francesco Sforza.

We followed the walk to the giant gates past the glorious fountain. At the ticket booth, I got out €10 – the fee then was €5 each.

The kind woman at the counter said "Quante anni hai – 62?"

What! I may be well over 62 but I think I look only 59. Then I saw that *cittadino anziano* got a discount.

"Gulp, yup that's me, an old lady and he is even older."

The tickets were only €3 each to visit a series of museums housed in the giant space. We were in art overload and loved it. The complex includes:

The *Pinacoteca del Castello Sforzesco*, paintings by giants like Canaletto, Tiepolo, Vincenzo Foppa, Titian and Tintoretto. (Anybody else make up stories about the models?)

The Museum of Ancient Art includes Michelangelo's last

sculpture, the *Rondanini Pietà*. (This was finished in 1564! No planned obsolescence here.)

The Museum of Musical Instruments. (Hmm, wonder if I could pluck out a tune on a lute.)

The Egyptian Museum. (We passed on this.)

The Prehistoric collections of the Archaeological Museum of Milan. (Yeah, we skipped that too.)

The Applied Arts Collection – this was interesting because contemporary furniture was included.

The Achille Bertarelli Print Collection. (We didn't see signs for this and couldn't find it.)

Later in the week, our next museum excursion was to Museo Del Novecento. Adjacent to the Duomo, we happened into it after once again hoping that a pazillion people weren't standing in the Duomo line. They were, so we got to see one of the largest national collections of Italian and international 20th century art – Futurism, Spatialism and lots of other isms. Picasso, Kandinsky and Matisse are hanging around too.

As we entered the building, I immediately thought of New York's Guggenheim Museum. The walkway to the galleries loops around and around and around. Ooops, getting dizzy just remembering it. Instead of looking at the art, like the Guggenheim, you are looking out huge windows facing Piazza Duomo. One space had floor to ceiling windows – each section framing great architecture. Brava!

Once we joined the gallery trail, we really had to pay attention to the signs pointing to the next space. The facility is huge and somehow we entered an adjacent building. When we were done, we giggled because we couldn't find our way out of the place.

Help!

Museo Poldi

Have I mentioned, everyone has visited Milan's Duomo – everyone but me? On yet another day we tried again. (When will I learn?) Sigh, maybe in December the lines will be shorter.

Time to seek out another tourist ignored gem - Museo Poldi Pezzoli.

Museo Poldi Pezzoli is tucked away on Via Manzoni 12. The museum was the home of a 19th Century Milanese nobleman, Gian Giacomo Poldi Pezzoli. When we went, tickets were €10.

Unless you are ageless anziani like Jack and I, then the tickets were €8.50. (Age has its benefits!)

They were filming something in the historic center of Milan that day and we couldn't walk past Teatro San Carlo. That meant we couldn't follow the directions on my phone to find the museum. *Errrggg*. Road blocks everywhere in the historic center. We tried the map. *Errrgg*.

Jack said follow me. I did. He found it. By now we were growling with hunger. Entering the museum doors, I asked the charming men working the desk if they had a restaurant. They didn't, but sent us up the street to the fabulous Ristorante Don Lisander.

It was elegant and the perfect way to transition from contemporary Milan to the glamour of the 19th century. The New York prices made me sad but the world class food and service turned the sad into glad.

Off to the museum! (I wondered if the staff thought we would really come back.) We bought our discounted tickets, turned to enter and gasped. An incredible neo-baroque fountain is nestled at the beginning of a grand staircase. The staircase guides folks to the rooms where Gian Giacomo lived.

The apartment is full of works by Botticelli, Bellini, Mantegna, Pollaiolo and others. The art just drew us all in. I spent quite a bit of time wondering who modeled for Sandro Botticelli's *Madonna of the Book*. Girlfriend, neighbor, courtesan? Twilight diffused light is kind of romantic.

Hmmm. Midge, it isn't too late to study a wee bit of art history.

The Murano Glass rooms, where you can also find portraits of our host, are chock full of Murano glass dating from the 15th to the 19th centuries. Unlike the faux Murano trinkets made in China one finds in Venice today, these were the real deal and glorious.

Want to skip a century or two? Giovani Battista Tiepolo's *Death of Saint Jerome* is worth some introspection.

In case you are running late and wonder what time it is, like the Mad Hatter you can dash into the Clock Room and check out the clocks dating from the 16th to 19th centuries. I wonder if Gian Giacomo was always on time or late for that important date?

Did you ever wonder why people collect what they collect?

Driving Home — Where are the Turbines?

I may have broken the bucolic mood of casual conversations with strangers by talking politics – but hey, there are things I want to know.

For instance, "Why," I asked a recent Milanese acquaintance, "don't I see one ugly faux power generating windmill on this pristine hill?"

Jack rolled his eyes. The woman looked at me like how could I not know the answer to that question and explained. "This is the north – the government is not like the government of the south."

That might have meant: our government ain't gonna let windmills ruin our tourist-loving views. We also talked about the *crisi* and the fact that jobs exist in the north but not the south – again different regional governments. The north has industry and the south doesn't.

Political conversation begone! (*Hmmm*, that is impossible.) Particularly since Jack and I drove a different route back to Pontelandolfo. As we drove south, my ire increased. We drove on A7 through the mountains in Liguria and noticed high tension electric lines transmitting power but not one giant windmill between Milan and Genoa. Not one.

Staring out the windows I realized that I also hadn't seen one gargantuan whirling edifice in the hills surrounding Lago Como, anywhere in the regions of Lombardia, Toscana or Lazio! Hmm, the trees were flowing in the wind. Perhaps that was an anomaly. Obviously, the wind has stopped blowing in Northern Italy. I'll bet those ski slopes never feel the slightest breeze. The hills of Rome must cry for a breath of wind. Years ago, cute Dutch looking windmills were used in Montefiesole, Tuscana for the salt production industry. But now, there obviously isn't enough wind to generate electricity or blow out a match.

Maybe driving around Italy isn't such a good idea for my psyche. Next time I will study the train schedules. We silly kids hadn't realized that our usual comfortable train ride to Milano was cheaper than driving.

Fernando shuddered as I thought that - driving is the perfect way to see Italy.

Biker Gang Rules the Highway!

Laughing and swapping sex tales, five of us celebrating the impending nuptials of Giusy were on our way to a glamorous spa. As we tooled down SS 87 towards Castelpetroso and our "ladies go wild day," I saw something up ahead that smacked the laugh off my face. I felt my stomach clutching. I swear, a threatening *vroom, vroom rumble* was floating through our open windows.

"Come si dice 'gang' in Italiano?" I asked.

"Gruppo," said Rossella.

"Anche gruppo di ragazzi cattivi?" I asked. Shit, how could creeps moving rapidly down the highway in tight formation be called a group?

From the back seat Annalaura, the youngest of us said, "Gang."

"Chiudi le sicure!" I screamed. I shuddered with fear and locked my door. "Merda," I continued. "What do we do if they block the highway and try to ravage us?" (Now, this simply could have been a 72-year-old's woo-woo fantasy. But really – who knows in today's mad world?)

It takes a lot to scare me, but fifteen to twenty men sporting tight red gang jackets getting their rocks off on *vroom-vroom* machines had taken over the highway ahead. Literally taken over the highway. They were riding five across and arrogantly blocking the lane.

Our car, now cautiously following only one car length behind, was filled with four gorgeous, scantily clad women and one old woman in her fourth act. The minute one of those men look in the mirror and see Rossella, Giusy, Annalaura and

Annarita, we are toast. How could we fend off an attack? I could try the *don't mess with the old crazy bitch* act. In my best Wicked Witch voice, with spit drooling from one side of my mouth and my fingers pointing I'll screech, "Beware, my red jacket friends! I'll put a curse on you that will dry up your sperm and shrink your dicks."

Hmm, how do I say that in Italian?

The women all stared at me and then started shrieking. Not in fear – in pure hysterical laughter! "Midge, ci sono dei vespisti!" they bellowed between laughs.

Vespisti? Like Wasps?

No, like old men riding Vespa scooters. We giggled. We laughed so hard that the car shook. I have seen hogs on the highway – motorcycle clubs racing around central New Jersey but never a bunch of primly seated men in red satin gang jackets on Vespas. Seated broomstick upright, helmets pointed directly to the sky, this group  of travelers backed the highway up for miles. Unlike the *vroom vroom* of motorcycles racing through the mountains, this was a *putt putt* of red turtles crawling east. They even had a service car with replacement vespas following them.

Anxious to get on our way, from inside our car with the windows now closed against their exhaust, we cursed them with such force that the leader felt the vibrations. Beware of five females filled with the blood of warriors sending the *malocchio.* The head red gave a signal and like red lemmings out to sea they all moved over to the right.

Great. Let's pass them. "How?" queried Rossella, who was driving, "the service car is straddling the middle line."

Time for a New Jersey Girl intervention. "Ride his ass," I said. Now, we were all going about 15 miles an hour, so this wasn't really a dangerous request. Plus, we all had seatbelts on and Covid vaccines. We were double safe.

Skeptical at first, Rossella got into the swing. Her glare. My glare. The glares from the back seat wafted to the rearview mirror of the sluggish service car. The driver pulled to the right.

Zap like a rocket launching at 16 miles an hour we roared around the service car and up the long line of vespisti. Soon we were sailing along to the spa. It is one straight thirty-minute shot from Pontelandolfo, but one feels like they are in a different place. The region of Molise is pristine – no garbage piles on the side of the road here. After driving through plains that alternate between industrial and agricultural uses, the mountains suddenly thrust up on our left.

As we got closer to Fonte del Benessere Resort and Centro Messèguè the gold magnificence of the Santuario di Maria SS. Addolorata practically blinded us. This massive cathedral high on a hill was created to honor the Virgin Mary's March 22, 1888 appearance.

I thanked her for getting us safely to the Spa and for changing road raging bikers into vespisti.

Arrest Him

We are driving through a neighboring town on our way to buy a new refrigerator. It is a glorious day. Blue sky, the sun is shining down on us.

"Jack that light is red."

"I can't see the light. The sun…"

"You just went through that red light."

"Maybe it doesn't work – those cars stopped too."

"They stopped so they wouldn't broadside us. Shit."

We head down the street when at the next intersection who should appear but *un carabiniere* – policeman – holding up a paletta, the very small yet very scary circle on a stick that means pull over or we shoot. They do carry guns. Sometimes they carry very big automatic guns.

Damn, we went through a stoplight and got caught. My stomach drops to my toes. Jack sits up straighter and assumes his remembered State Police posture. I roll down my window and smile – cripes, I am seventy-two years old, flirting ain't gonna work – maybe dimwitted old lady?

"Buon Giorno," I say with a smile.

Jack follows my lead, "Buon Giorno."

The police officer does not crack a smile, "Patente e libretto."

I open the glove box and tons of *scontrini* – receipts – fall out. I find not one but two plastic folders holding documents. I drop the blue one. I feel the police officer staring at me. I open the black folder but haven't a clue what I am looking for. What is *il libretto* – is that the registration? He touches my hand – I freeze. He points. I give him the grey thing he points at. It must be il libretto.

The carabinieri always seem to work in twos. The rear of the police car was open and a computer appeared. The second officer grabs il libretto, which when I read it later was the registration, and started typing away. Rats, I think there goes another ticket to the car. The car that is in my name driven by Jack who couldn't see the freakin' red light.

By now I have the insurance and our international driver's licenses ready for him.

"I documenti per favore."

I try to give him the international driver's licenses – he pushes them aside. He doesn't care about the insurance either.

"I vostri passaporti!" He says a bit severely.

We are so screwed. Here we go on a slow boat back to the United States. Or worse, the computer-generated phone hell of the American Consulate. I realize he needs to know we are Italian citizens and live in Pontelandolfo half the year. The problem is I need to get out of the car. All those car stops we have seen on the USA news demonstrate how dangerous it is to get out of the car. But my purse is on the back seat. What to do? My grandmother leaps into my body and suddenly my Italian improves two hundred percent.

"Siamo cittadini italiani. Residenza a Pontelandolfo. Potrei uscire dalla macchina. La mia borsa è sul sedile dietro."

I get out of the car, look directly into his handsome brown eyes and wish I was twenty-five. Then I go to the back seat and get my purse. Opening my wallet to get my residence card demonstrates that I happen to have a wee bit of cash too. I quickly take out my carta d'identità and gesture to Jack to take out his.

While Jack arches up in the seat to get his wallet, I say. "Viviamo a Pontelandolfo sei mesi all' anno e in New Jersey altri sei mesi."

"I speak a little inglese. Where in New Jersey."

"Tu parli bene l'inglese," I say. "Siamo a Ewing vicino Philadelphia."

He nods. I smile. He speaks English about as well as I

speak Italian, but hey, compliments go a long way. He takes our identification cards back to the computer. Somehow, I don't feel as frightened. Jack is still staring straight ahead.

He comes back and doesn't look happy. "To drive in Italy avete bisogno della patente internazionale."

He throws Jack's New Jersey license back at him. What the #@%&!, I think. Why did Jack give him his license – all he wanted was his residence card. I leap into my "Ms Fixit" role.

"Mi scusi signore, abbiamo le patenti internazionali. Sono queste." I hand him the same two grey international driver's licenses that I tried to give him earlier. We get them every year from AAA and have never shown them to anyone in ten years. Are these acceptable or do we end up in the cop car? He doesn't even open them – just hands them back and goes back to the computer. I get back in the car. If they want to arrest us it will take a crane to pull me out of the car. I am prepping for my 1960's dead weight protest mode.

He slowly walks back. I slowly tighten my muscles and slump lower into the car. Jack sits up even taller. The policeman looks at me and pauses. I cringe.

"Buon fine settimana segnori," he says with a smile.

I smile. He turns and walks away. Jack starts the car. I wave at the policemen. Thank you, we will have a good weekend. But first, let's go buy that refrigerator.

Epilogue

Now what? Do I keep on driving? Is it time to look at smart cars or anything smaller than an oversized but comfortable Fiat 500L? Sitting here in my writer's room, Bar Elimar on Piazza Roma, sipping my perfect cappuccino, I've been trying to come up with the button that closes this collection of stories and propels me onto the next project. Watching the band of aged men slapping cards down on the next table with angst or joy as they play scopa, I realized that as long as we spend half of the year in Pontelandolfo the stories will continue to smack me in the face. How can I not scribble down the joys, foibles, and views that I see?

Daily, the Sannio Hills reveal a person, place or event that is a story unto itself. Maybe it is because I grew up in New Jersey, but my DNA was lusting for Pontelandolfo, or maybe it is because I am in my third act, but whatever the reason living in Southern Italy, the creative juices flow. Sometimes they overflow as I try to dash out my blog, pitch a play, finish a cookbook or continue on the memoir track.

"Negozia di Cina," sold for less than one-euro, are tiny little pink, black and white plaid cloth bound notebooks. (Why were they ever covered in that? Maybe they were part of the old "Hello Kitty" merch?)

Who would buy these mini books shrink wrapped in evil plastic? I did. They were cheap. I bought a box. No more cumbersome than a big matchbox, I have filled at least seventy-five of them in the eight plus years we have been splitting our time between the USA and Italy. Recipes, snippets of conversations, wisdom of the village elders, email addresses, telephone numbers without names, impressions and rants filled the pages. These notebooks are in my pockets, pocketbooks, and stuffed in my desk. As I sit in the bar, surrounded by the energy that is Italy, and write a blog, *Nonna's Mulberry Tree*, about one of the gems or not so shiny gems found in the notes, I rip out the pages.

WOW, that felt good. Blog post done and note tossed.

Honk, beep. I realized a few years back that these tiny jotters were full of car stories. Growing up in rural New Jersey, cars were an important part of our lives. Need a loaf of bread – hop in the car. Dancing lessons – hop in the car. Family night out at the drive in – sleep in the car. Cars have always been a part of my existence, however, their uses changed depending on the who, what, where and acts of my life.

The Nash Rambler that carried my first act friends and I from Montclair State to Stevens Tech fraternities could tell stories that would have sent our parents into a spiral.

My bright red Ford Maverick was totaled by one of my drama students out to buy supplies for our high school production of *The Wizard of OZ*.

My Impala, called the "pimp mobile" by my friends, took me out of teaching in a public high school to an arts-based career that I have enjoyed immensely.

As I think about it, cars have been with me through every act of my life. Cripes, I wonder if they have a one-person-fourth-act transport car that can zoom up steep hills and wend its way in donkey width roads? The little plaid notebooks have only found their way into my heart during this act. I will continue to drive and continue to fill notebooks – learning from both.

Now, thanks to our family of Fiats and my writing, we have – no make that *I have* - been learning to accept what life tosses at me. Annually, when we head back to Italy, I try not to pack my type A personality and just leave it hidden in a New Jersey closet. I do pack more pens. Our Fernando Fiat 500 L purrs when we appear and rescue him/her from the Italian storage garage. The little notebooks leap into my pocket. They know life with Midge and Jack in a picturesque Italian village will always be an adventure. Stories will be unearthed and shared.

Quest'è Italia!
Ci Vediamo!

Tired of waiting outside Bar Elimar for his owner, Midge, Fernando slowly jiggles the wire to the horn. **Honk!** *Maybe Midge will slug back her Campari, close her computer and take me home. Or not...*

Nothing like a shine to perk up Fernando's day. "Hey, watch it, Giovanni - that curly rag tickles."

Acknowledgements

It really does take a village! In my case it took two villages to make *Cars, Castles, Cows and Chaos* a reality. Thank you to my family, and friends who are like family, in New Jersey and Pontelandolfo, Italy.

Team Jersey Girl has had my back for many a project. Ace critic, Kathy Hall – who loves to diagram a sentence – gives all my work its first read and sounds the alarm for things that need to change. Maryann Carroll, who I have begged to be my agent, reads, dissects and discusses. Alexandra Rose Niedt, my precious niece, is my best cheerleader and pulls me out of the depths of "will this work" despair. When it comes to editing my drafts, my 16 years of Catholic education and incredibly tolerant husband, Jack Huber, is quick on the red ink draw. Marie Lawrence, Bruce Donaldson, Regina Hayes and Susan Guerrera Niedt were my first readers and told me what was funny, boring, great and just plain stupid.

Janet Cantore-Watson is a very special member of Team Jersey Girl. She not only did the illustrations for the book, is a hell of an actress, but has been a fighter in my artistic corner for over fifty years.

The Pontelandolfo Crew has fed me, swapped tales, dragged me from adventure to adventure and provided me the emotional support it takes to lock myself in my office and write. Grazie mille to the entire Mancini family with special hugs to Rossella and Annarita Mancini. Bar Elimar on Piazza Roma has let me sit at a table for hours, stare at the piazza and type. All you subscribers to my blog about Pontelandolfo, *Nonna's Mulberry Tree*, don't realize how the comments you make to my blog posts nudge me on.

The biggest of thanks go to the publishers that embraced my work and made me realize that in my second act I could redefine myself. Read Furiously is an amazing company and has been great to work with. Samantha Atzeni and Adam Wilson provided nurturing support for this first collection of memoir-esque short stories. Thank you for believing in me.

And a very special thanks to anyone I forgot to thank.

Midge Guerrera, with her ever patient husband, Jack, spends half the year on a farm in Italy and the other half in a New Jersey high-rise. Her work has been published by Next Stage Press, Applause Theatre and Cinema Books, New Jersey Performing Arts Center Learning Guides, Anchorage Press, and the American Alliance for Theatre in Education.

Her blog, www.nonnasmulberrytree.com, features the food, fun and foibles of being a part-time expat in Pontelandolfo, a small Southern Italian village.

You can learn more about Midge's work at
www.midgeguerrera.com

A Note to our Furious Readers

From all of us at Read Furiously, we hope you enjoyed our latest title, *Cars, Castles, Cows, and Chaos.*

There are countless narratives in this world and we would like to share as many of them as possible with our Furious Readers.

It is with this in mind that we pledge to donate a portion of these book sales to causes that are special to Read Furiously and those involved in *Cars, Castles, Cows, and Chaos.* These causes are chosen with the intent to better the lives of others who are struggling to tell their own stories.

Reading is more than a passive activity – it is the opportunity to play an active role within our world. At Read Furiously, its editors and its creators wish to add an active voice to the world we all share because we believe any growth within the company is aimless if we can't also nurture positive change in our local and global communities. The causes we support are culturally and socially conscious to encourage a sense of civic responsibility associated with the act of reading. Each cause has been researched thoroughly, discussed openly, and voted upon carefully by our team of Read Furiously editors.

To find out more about who, what, why, and where Read Furiously lends its support, please visit our website at readfuriously.com/charity

Happy reading and giving, Furious Readers!

Read Often, Read Well, Read Furiously!

Look for these other great titles from

Read Often. Read Well.

Poetry
All These Little Stars
Silk City Sparrow
Dear Terror
Whatever you Thought, Think Again
Until the Roof Lifted Off

Essays and Anthologies
Stay Salty: Life in the Garden State
We don't do "just okay" anymore
Furious Lit vol 1: Tell Me A Story
The World Takes: Life in the Garden State
Putting Out: Essays on Otherness
Working Through This

The One 'n Done Series
Helium
Brethren Hollow
Girls, They'll Never Take Us Alive
What About Tuesday
The Legend of Dave Bradley

Graphic Novels
Pursuit: A Collection of Artwork
In the Fallout
Brian & Bobbi
The MOTHER Principle

Children's Books
The Little Gray Witch